P9-EMB-716

ORGANIZATIONAL IMPROVEMENT
AND
ACCOUNTABLILITY

LESSONS FOR EDUCATION FROM OTHER SECTORS

Brian Stecher and Sheila Nataraj Kirby

EDITORS

Prepared for
The William and Flora Hewlett Foundation

 EDUCATION

The research described in this report was prepared for The William and Flora Hewlett Foundation by RAND Education.

Library of Congress Cataloging-in-Publication Data

Organizational improvement and accountability : lessons for education from other sectors / Brian Stecher ... [et al.].
    p. cm.
    "MG-136."
    Includes bibliographical references.
    ISBN 0-8330-3500-2 (paperback)
    1. Educational accountability—United States. 2. School management and organization—United States. 3. Organizational effectiveness—Evaluation. I. Stecher, Brian M. II. Rand Corporation.

  LB2806.22.O74 2004
  379.1'58—dc22

                                                   2003024743

The RAND Corporation is a nonprofit research organization providing objective analysis and effective solutions that address the challenges facing the public and private sectors around the world. RAND's publications do not necessarily reflect the opinions of its research clients and sponsors.

RAND® is a registered trademark.

Cover design by Peter Soriano

Published 2004 by the RAND Corporation
1700 Main Street, P.O. Box 2138, Santa Monica, CA 90407-2138
1200 South Hayes Street, Arlington, VA 22202-5050
201 North Craig Street, Suite 202, Pittsburgh, PA 15213-1516
RAND URL: http://www.rand.org/
To order RAND documents or to obtain additional information, contact
Distribution Services: Telephone: (310) 451-7002;
Fax: (310) 451-6915; Email: order@rand.org

Preface

Educational accountability became the law of the land with the passage of the No Child Left Behind Act of 2001. As states rushed to develop accountability systems that met the requirements of the new law, the Hewlett Foundation asked RAND Education to undertake two tasks. The first was to write a paper that delineated carefully the provisions of the new law and the underlying assumptions on which the new test-based accountability systems are based, and to disseminate it broadly to experts and practitioners. With help from a group of experts who participated in an Accountability Forum held at RAND in 2002, we produced a RAND Corporation White Paper, *Working Smarter to Leave No Child Behind: Practical Insights for School Leaders* (Stecher, Hamilton, and Gonzalez, 2003).

The second task we undertook was to examine models of accountability in sectors other than education. The goal of the investigation was to understand how such models work and their applicability to education. This monograph documents the results of that examination. It should be of interest to educational policymakers, educational administrators, and others who are interested in improving the effectiveness of schools. The work was sponsored by the William and Flora Hewlett Foundation.

Contents

Figure and Tables

Figure

Tables

Summary

Performance-Based Accountability in Education

In December 2001, the U.S. Congress approved a reauthorization of the Elementary and Secondary Education Act (ESEA) and renamed it the "No Child Left Behind Act" (P.L. 107-110, H.R. 1). The cornerstone of the No Child Left Behind Act (NCLB) is a performance-based accountability system built around student test results. This increased emphasis on accountability represents an important change from past federal educational initiatives, which focused primarily on the provision of services. Supporters of NCLB argued that previous educational reforms were unsuccessful in large measure because they ignored student outcomes. Borrowing from successful private-sector management practices, they made the case that student achievement would only improve when educators were judged in terms of student performance and consequences were attached to the results.

Three basic elements make up the performance-based accountability system required by NCLB: goals; assessments for measuring the attainment of goals and judging success; and consequences (rewards or sanctions). The goals are embodied in a set of content or performance standards that schools and teachers use to guide curriculum and instruction. Tests are developed to measure student learning and determine whether students have mastered the standards. Improved performance on the tests leads to rewards that are intended to reinforce effective behavior; poor performance on the tests leads to sanctions and improvement efforts that are intended to modify ineffective behavior. Some of the incentives operate through parents. If a child's school is deemed to be in need of improvement, parents can request a transfer to another school and/or supplemental educational services from private providers.

As clear as these procedures may seem, the key principles underlying NCLB accountability are largely untested in education. The mechanisms through which the system is intended to work to improve student achievement and eliminate failing schools are not well understood. In this environment, decisionmakers at the state, district, and school levels are looking for guidance to help them make their systems as effective as possible. One place to look for possible insights into effective accountability mechanisms is outside the educational sector. The purpose of this project is to examine accountability in other fields to find lessons that might be relevant for educators.

Accountability in Other Sectors

We cast our net widely before selecting specific instances of accountability to study. We solicited recommendations from educational researchers as well as research colleagues who study organizations in other fields. We also reviewed the debate within education surrounding the passage of NCLB for references to accountability in other domains. The final set of cases reflects our desire to present examples that are relevant, interesting, and diverse. Our sample includes cases from both the manufacturing and service sectors. In each case, we tried to understand the processes through which providers are held accountable, how well these processes have worked, and whether they might be applicable to education.

We examined five accountability models:

- Two accountability models drawn from the manufacturing sector (although now spreading to service industries): the Malcolm Baldrige National Quality Award Program and the Toyota Production System (TPS). Strictly speaking, these are models of organizational improvement set within the larger context of market accountability rather than full-fledged accountability systems. Both, however, offer ways to improve organizational efficiency.

- A performance incentive model used in the evaluation of job training programs for the poor established by the Job Training Partnership Act (JTPA) of 1982 (now replaced by the Workforce Investment Act (WIA) of 1998).
- Accountability in the legal sector. The legal accountability model is largely based on notions of "professional accountability," which entail controlling entry into the profession, mandatory capacity-building, self-policing, and protecting client concerns.
- Accountability in health care. We explored three aspects of health care accountability that seemed particularly relevant for education: clinical practice guidelines, use of statistical risk adjustment methods, and the public reporting of health performance measures.

These models differ in terms of their comprehensiveness, effectiveness, and applicability to education. In this monograph, we describe each model, summarize the relevant research on effectiveness, and draw specific lessons for educators.

Implications for Education

We recognize that the education sector has unique characteristics that set it apart from the other sectors we examined. Yet we believe the analyses of these different accountability models offer useful insights on ways to enhance system-wide accountability in education, including how to improve the operation of schools and districts to achieve higher performance. Specific lessons learned for education include the following:

Broaden performance measures. Educators should be careful when setting performance objectives because the objectives will drive behavior—for better or for worse. Broadening "what counts" in the system is one way to diffuse the pressure to focus too narrowly and to deemphasize other important priorities.

Make sure performance goals are fair to all students and schools. The accountability system should establish reasonable improvement targets for all schools and should not reward or penalize schools or districts for factors beyond their control. The goal of fair comparisons also needs to be balanced against the goal of closing the gap between successful and unsuccessful students. Nevertheless, the experiences of JTPA/WIA and health point out the advantages of performance targets that are sensitive to initial inputs.

Develop standards of practice in promising areas and encourage professional accountability. Movements to create more-explicit standards of practice would foster professional accountability and provide guidance to help schools and districts improve their performance. We encourage educators to select promising areas in which more-detailed practice guidelines might be developed. Such guidelines can form the basis for more-detailed standards for the teaching profession so teachers can be more aggressive about monitoring their own professional competence. These steps would help broaden and deepen accountability in education.

Develop an integrated, comprehensive strategy to help schools and districts improve their performance. This research points to four key elements of an improvement strategy:

- Undertaking a focused institutional self-assessment (including asking the right questions and assembling the right kinds of information)
- Understanding the school system as a linked process
- Developing and applying an expanded knowledge base about effective practice in varying situations
- Empowering participants in the process (notably teachers) to contribute to improvement efforts.

Developing and adopting such a strategy in education will require time, effort, and a willingness to adapt principles from outside the educational sector. Pilot efforts to adapt and test these components in diverse schools settings and focused efforts to create educational applications would be a good starting place to try to take advantage of the successful experiences of other sectors.

In Conclusion

This investigation of accountability in other sectors sharpens our thinking about accountability in education. It suggests ways in which educators can develop better strategies for improving the performance of schools and districts and policymakers can redefine educational accountability to make it more effective. It is worth pointing out that, although education has much in common with business, law, and health care, it faces unique challenges that other sectors do not face. Nevertheless, educators have much to learn from these other fields. In the end, they will have to develop an accountability model that addresses their unique situation. However, there is much they can draw on from accountability efforts outside of education.

Acknowledgments

We are particularly grateful for the help we received from Jennifer Li, who worked with us to make the presentations consistent across chapters. We want to thank Cynthia Cook and Paul Shekelle for their helpful reviews of the manuscript and their excellent suggestions of additional sources of information. We also want to thank Jorge Ruiz-de-Velasco, Marshall Smith, and the William and Flora Hewlett Foundation for their patience and support as the task grew larger than originally anticipated.

CHAPTER ONE

Introduction

Sheila Nataraj Kirby and Brian Stecher

Accountability in Education

Accountability in education refers to the practice of holding educational systems responsible for the quality of their products—students' knowledge, skills, and behaviors. It is neither a new idea nor a new practice. In fact, Kirst (1990), in his historical overview of educational accountability, points out that as far back as mid–19th century England, schools were paid according to the performance of their students on standardized examinations—"payment by results." In 20th century America, public schools were held accountable through a variety of regulatory mechanisms—school buildings had to meet strict safety codes, teachers had to obtain formal certification, students had to study from approved textbooks, and a cornucopia of specific programs was mandated by state and federal governments. Schools were required to comply with these rules to ensure that students received an adequate education.

As the 21st century begins, educational accountability has taken a different turn. In December 2001, the U.S. Congress approved a reauthorization of the Elementary and Secondary Education Act (ESEA) and renamed it the "No Child Left Behind Act" (P.L. 107-110, H.R. 1). The cornerstone of the No Child Left Behind Act (NCLB) is an emphasis on accountability based on student test results. Supporters of test-based accountability argue that previous reforms failed because they focused on inputs (e.g., facilities, teachers, textbooks) or on specific practices (e.g., remedial instruction, health services, school lunch programs), but never on outcomes. Advocates of NCLB further contend that educators have never been held responsible for student learning; instead teachers and administrators are paid (i.e., rewarded) on the basis of their educational backgrounds and their longevity in the profession. As a result, they feel no personal or collective responsibility for how much students learn. Borrowing from successful private-sector management practices, accountability advocates believe that student achievement will improve only when educators are judged in terms of student performance and experience consequences as a result.

Although the No Child Left Behind act is hundreds of pages long and the details of its implementation are quite complex, the logic of its accountability system is quite simple. The accountability system has three major components:

- Goals—explicit statements of desired student performance—to convey clear and shared expectations for all parties
- Assessments for measuring attainment of goals and judging success
- Consequences (rewards or sanctions) to motivate administrators, teachers, and students to maximize effort and effectiveness.

Figure 1.1 shows how these elements work together. The goals of the system are embodied in a set of content or performance standards that schools and teachers use to guide curriculum and instruction. Tests are developed to measure student learning and determine whether students have mastered the standards. Improved performance on the tests leads to rewards that reinforce effective behavior; poor performance on the tests leads to sanctions and improvement efforts that modify ineffective behavior. The actual NCLB rules are a more complex version of this basic model.

A few of the specific details of NCLB are worth mentioning because they pervade the discussion of the reform. Accountability comes in the forms of increasing annual goals for student achievement and

Figure 1.1
Elements of a Standards-Based Accountability Model

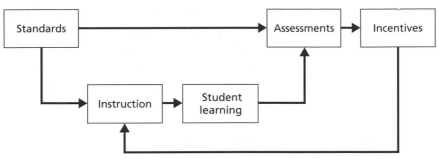

RAND *MG136-1.1*

escalating incentives for schools and districts based on student achievement. NCLB requires that, by 2014, *all* students must be proficient in reading and mathematics based on state-adopted tests. Schools and districts must make *adequate yearly progress* (AYP) toward meeting these targets. Furthermore, the same annual targets must be met by students in every significant population subgroup, including racial and ethnic groups, socioeconomic groups, and special education students. Although some of the Act's strictest sanctions apply only to Title I schools (low-income schools that are eligible for extra resources under Title I of ESEA/NCLB), the major accountability provisions of NCLB affect all the nation's public K–12 schools, including charter schools.

NCLB couples greater accountability for student performance with increased local control and flexibility. It emphasizes high-quality teachers using scientifically based practices and expanded options for parents. While the NCLB accountability system is multilevel, involving state policymakers, district leaders, school staff, and local parents, the state has the least-active role in the improvement process. Instead, the primary responsibility for improvement is assigned to the local level, i.e., the individual school or the district, rather than to the state government, as was the case in the past. NCLB also establishes minimum standards for teacher quality (and for the qualifications of instructional aides) and mandates that schools use scientifically based practices to promote student achievement. Another important feature of NCLB is its emphasis on the right of parents to make decisions about how and where their children are educated. If schools are not doing well, parents can request that their child be transferred to another school or be given supplemental educational services from a private provider. To exercise their options, parents must be informed annually about the professional qualifications of their children's teachers, about the success of their school, and about the performance of their child.

Other Approaches to Educational Accountability[1]

The standards-based approach embodied in NCLB is not the only way to hold schools accountable. Several other approaches exist, sometimes simultaneously, in public education (Finn (2002); O'Day (2002); Darling-Hammond (1991); Adams and Kirst (1998)). For example, Adams and Kirst (1998) describe six types of educational accountability: *bureaucratic accountability, legal accountability, professional accountability, political accountability, moral accountability,* and *market- or choice-based accountability*. The accountability models are defined by the way they answer four key questions:

- Who is held accountable?
- For what are they held accountable?
- To whom are they accountable?
- What are the consequences of failing to meet the goals that are set for them?

Table 1.1 compares and contrasts four models of accountability. In the NCLB version of performance-based accountability, schools and districts are the units that are held accountable. The district monitors the performance of schools and is responsible for taking

---

[1] Because we are interested mainly in accountability in other sectors, we provide here only a brief overview of types of educational accountability. Interested readers should consult several very good articles that provide a more detailed examination of the advantages and disadvantages of these various types of accountability in education (see Adams and Kirst, 1998; Darling-Hammond, 1991; and O'Day, 2002); and digests provided by ERIC at http://eric-web.tc.columbia.edu.

Table 1.1
Overview of Key Features of Educational Accountability

Models of accountability	Who is held accountable?	To whom are they held accountable?	For what are they accountable?	What are the consequences of failing to meet goals?
Performance- or test-based accountability	School/ district	State/federal government	Raising student proficiency (in NCLB, it is measured by standardized tests)	Increasingly severe sanctions (e.g., student transfer, supplemental services, reconstitution)
Bureaucratic accountability	School/ district	State	Compliance with rules and regulations	Sanctions such as loss of accreditation, firing of principals/ teachers
Professional accountability	Teachers	Professional peers/ professional organizations	Following recognized professional practices	Professional sanctions; loss of certification
Market accountability	School	Parents	Academic standards, philosophical/ religious norms, student discipline, other features	Loss of students, leading to loss of revenue, economic failure

action if they are not performing adequately. The state monitors the performance of districts, and the federal government monitors the performance of the states. Schools must meet increasing targets for student proficiency based on standards-based test scores. If schools fail to meet their targets, they face increasingly severe sanctions. After two years, the district must provide transportation to another school for students who want to leave. After three years, it must provide supplemental educational services from outside providers. Ultimately, the school staff can be replaced and the school reconstituted.

Under bureaucratic accountability—the norm in the recent past—rules and regulations specify how districts, schools, and teachers are to behave. Various public agencies review school performance and monitor compliance. Bureaucratic accountability makes implicit assumptions that both policy and practice can be standardized, i.e., policymakers can devise general rules and create broad program initiatives that make sense for all schools, and teachers can apply general instructional principles that make sense for all students. Under these assumptions, it makes sense to use regulatory and inspection systems to minimize noncompliance. If districts or schools do not follow regulations, they may be sanctioned, e.g., suffer loss of accreditation or removal of administrators.

Professional accountability is built on the assumption that teachers are professionals who possess sufficient expertise to determine the best ways of meeting the individual needs of their students. Thus, professional competence and standards for professional practice become important. Professional teacher organizations have a major role in establishing such standards. Quality is ensured through accreditation of teacher preparation schools, certification and licensure of teachers, and requirements for continuous professional development. Failing to meet professional standards could result in loss of certification and/or disciplinary proceedings similar to those in the legal or medical professions. There is considerable debate, however, about whether the knowledge base for teacher education is developed enough to embody in explicit standards for practice and/or whether the current certification and licensure processes ensure the "quality" of teachers.

As the name implies, market accountability uses the interaction between consumers (parents) and providers (schools) to regulate practice and ensure quality. In a market system, parents are allowed to select the schools their children attend rather than their children being assigned to schools based on where they live. A variety of schemes exists for bringing market mechanisms to education, including vouchers, charter schools, and magnet programs. In voucher systems, parents receive vouchers that they can use to purchase educational services (much as the federal government subsidizes food consumption through food stamps). In magnet or charter school programs, individual schools are freed from some regulations and are given some ability to compete directly with each other for students. The underlying theory is that competition among schools will lead to higher quality. Good schools will be successful; underperforming schools will be driven out as they lose students and revenue. However, even under ideal conditions, choice alone is not enough to guarantee full accountability in terms of ensuring a quality education for all students because of issues of supply, access, and information (Gill, Timpane, Ross, and Brewer, 2001).

These four accountability models need not exist in isolation from one another, and in practice they seldom do. For example, the NCLB standards-based accountability model is layered on top of existing bureaucratic provisions. Obviously, some of these models can create tensions when implemented in combination. For example, professional accountability, which emphasizes the authority and knowledge of individual teachers, is diametrically opposed to the traditional form of bureaucratic accountability, which attempts to minimize the role of the teacher in decisionmaking. However, many authors advocate combining elements of several models to mitigate the negative effects associated with individual models. For example, Finn (2002) advocates combining standards-based or test-based accountability with market accountability whereas O'Day (2002) suggests that the weakness of professional accountability could be alleviated to some extent by combining it with test-based accountability. In fact, NCLB itself includes some aspects of these other models. For example, the school choice provisions embody a market-based approach, and the mandates for scientifically based programs and highly qualified teachers entail a form of professional accountability.

Accountability in Other Sectors

Many of the key principles underlying NCLB—e.g., universal testing, parental choice—are largely untested in education, and the mechanisms by which these principles should work to improve student achievement and eliminate failing schools are not well understood. In this environment, decisionmakers at the state, local, and school levels are looking for guidance to help them make their systems as effective as possible. One place to look for possible insights about effective accountability mechanisms is outside the educational sector.

The purpose of this project was to examine accountability in other fields to see what lessons educators might learn. We cast our net widely, examining cases from both the manufacturing and service sectors, first to understand how providers are held accountable in those sectors and next to examine evidence on how well these accountability processes worked. Our selection process was thoughtful but not comprehensive. We solicited recommendations from educational researchers as well as research colleagues who study organizations in other fields. We reviewed the debate within education surrounding the passage of NCLB for references to accountability in other domains. The final set of cases reflects our desire to present examples that are relevant, interesting, and diverse. The reader will have to judge whether these objectives were met.

The five "cases" we investigated were the Malcolm Baldrige National Quality Award Program, the Toyota Production System (TPS)/Lean Manufacturing, the Job Training Partnership Act (JTPA) of 1982 and its successor the Workforce Investment Act (WIA), the legal profession, and selected aspects of the U.S. health care system. The Baldrige Awards and the Toyota Production System are easily classified as market-based accountability systems; the connection between consumers and providers is clear and direct. Firms and providers producing goods and services in a competitive environment are likely to be successful only to the extent that they satisfy the needs of consumers. In the JTPA, performance-based incentives are used to increase efficiency by tying payments to direct measures of output. Both the legal and medical cases involve markets to an extent, but they are markets in which consumers cannot judge quality as easily. As a result, both domains have seen the rise of intermediaries or professional organizations that attempt to provide information on quality. This brings aspects of professional accountability to both domains. The health care case is also relevant to performance-based accountability, because the health profession is far ahead of education in defining and measuring standards of practice. Since education has elements of market-based accountability, performance-based accountability, and professional accountability, we believe these cases may offer useful insights for educators.

Organization of the Monograph

Chapters Two and Three discuss two accountability models drawn from the manufacturing sector (although they are now spreading to service industries): the Malcolm Baldrige National Quality Award Program and the Toyota Production System/Lean Manufacturing. Strictly speaking, these are models of organizational improvement set within the larger context of market accountability, not full-fledged accountability systems; both offer a way to improve organizational efficiency. Chapter Four describes the experience of JTPA and WIA, which set performance-based goals and incentives for centers providing employment-related training. It offers important lessons for the performance incentive provisions of the NCLB. Chapter Five provides an overview of how professional accountability operates in the legal profession. Chapters Six through Eight look at aspects of accountability in the health care system. We explore three aspects of health care accountability that seem particularly relevant for education: clinical practice guidelines, use of risk adjustment models, and the public reporting of health performance measures and its impact on providers and consumers.

These five models differ widely both in terms of comprehensiveness and in their applicability to education. As a result, the chapters vary in depth and detail, but all attempt to draw implications for the education sector. We hope they help educators think about a number of specific issues, including how to make their goals and expectations clearer, how to use data as a basis for improvement, how to make use of multiple measures, how to adjust for the heterogeneity of inputs, and how to establish standards for practice. We will return to these themes in the final summary chapter.

CHAPTER TWO
Malcolm Baldrige National Quality Award Program

Sheila Nataraj Kirby

The goal of the Malcolm Baldrige National Quality Act of 1987 (Public Law 100-107) is to establish criteria for performance excellence and to provide organizations a framework for designing, implementing, and assessing a process for managing all business operations to be able to meet those criteria. Given that many schools and districts are struggling to improve themselves and the performance of their students, it seemed a useful exercise to examine the Malcolm Baldrige National Quality Award (MBNQA) to see what lessons it might hold for education. This chapter describes the MBNQA Program, its criteria for performance excellence, and the evidence that exists regarding the link between implementation of the MBNQA framework and operating performance. We then discuss how these criteria have been applied to the educational sector and the experiences of two school districts that were recent winners of the award. The last section provides some implications for the use of MBNQA within the NCLB educational accountability context.

We should note that there are several quality awards—for example, the Deming Prize in Japan, the European Quality Award (EQA), and the Australian Quality Award (AQA)—each of which is based on a perceived model of total quality management. Although there are some differences among the quality awards, they provide a universal audit framework for evaluating management practice, quality of methods, techniques, and tools, deployment of quality plans, and results (Ghobadian and Woo, 1996).[1] We have neither the expertise nor the resources to evaluate these different awards or frameworks to see which one is the "best." Our decision to focus on the Baldrige award was therefore based not on evaluative criteria but on our judgment that, because it is widely accepted in the United States (not only in manufacturing or business), it seemed an appropriate avenue to explore for lessons that might be applicable to the educational sector.

Background

Since the 1980s, Total Quality Management (TQM) has emerged as one of the most significant and pervasive developments in U.S. business practice. Powell (1995), citing Ross (1993), describes TQM as:

> An integrated management philosophy and set of practices that emphasizes, among other things, continuous improvement, meeting customers' requirements, reducing rework, long-range thinking, increased employee involvement and teamwork, process redesign, competitive benchmarking, team-based problem-solving, constant measurement of results, and closer relationships with suppliers. (p. 16)

Easton and Jarrell (1998) point out that the focus on TQM began in 1980 primarily in manufacturing companies that were facing strong global competition from Japan. TQM was widely credited with leading the revolution in industry that led to Japan's rise to global prominence in the postwar years (see Powell, 1995). The U.S. TQM movement gained momentum in 1987 with the establishment

---

[1] Ghobadian and Woo (1996) provide an excellent comparison of the characteristics of these four major quality awards, pointing out, for example, that—unlike the other three—the Deming Prize is not based on an underlying framework linking concepts and practices to results. Thus, it does not assume causality but is more prescriptive in that it recommends a list of desirable quality-oriented "best practices," such as quality circles and standardization. The MBNQA, EQA, and AQA are based on an underlying causal framework linking different constituents of quality management and are prescriptive in the sense that they expound a particular philosophy of good management. However, they do not recommend particular methods or tools.

of the Baldrige Award program by Congress "to recognize U.S. organizations for their achievements in quality and performance and to raise awareness about the importance of quality and performance excellence as a competitive edge" (see http://www.nist.gov/public_affairs/factsheet/baldfaqs.html). The award recognizes performance excellence in each of five following categories: manufacturing, service, small business, and, starting in 1999, education and health care. Up to three awards may be given in each category each year, although in some areas and some years, no awards are given if applicants are judged as not meeting standards. The award is not given for a specific product or service but for meeting the Baldrige criteria for performance excellence.

The U.S. Commerce Department's National Institute of Standards and Technology (NIST) manages the MBNQA program with assistance from the American Society for Quality, a professional nonprofit association. The award program is a joint government/private-sector effort. Private-sector and state and local organizations have contributed over $100 million, including $10 million raised by private industry to help launch the program, and the time and efforts of hundreds of largely private-sector volunteers. The volunteers serve as members of the Board of Examiners to review applications, make site visits, and make recommendations regarding awards. The board comprises more than 300 experts from industry, educational institutions, governments at all levels, and nonprofit organizations, who go through a training process to become Baldrige examiners. The federal government provides about $5 million annually to NIST to manage the program. Application fees are charged to cover expenses associated with distribution and review of applications and development of feedback reports. The application fees range from $5,000 for large organizations to $500 for nonprofit education institutions.

Organizations that wish to apply submit an Eligibility Determination Package to establish eligibility in one of the five award categories. Once they are determined to be eligible, they submit a completed application form along with an application report consisting of an organizational overview and responses to the Criteria for Performance Excellence. All applications go through an independent review by examiners; some are selected for consensus review by a panel of judges (stage 1). Based on the consensus review, some are selected for a site visit review (stage 2). Stage 3 consists of the site visits, review, and recommendations for winners. All applicants receive a detailed feedback report regardless of what stage they reach in the process. The feedback report is a written assessment of the organization's strengths and vulnerabilities and contains detailed, actionable comments on opportunities for improvement. NIST estimates that applicants receive approximately 300 hours of feedback each from expert examiners while organizations that are chosen for a site visit receive over 1,000 hours of review.[2] Several winners of the award have praised the quality and usefulness of the feedback.[3]

Another important emphasis of the program is dissemination. Recipients of the award are asked to participate in the annual conference at which the awards are announced, and several of them have cosponsored regional conferences. They are also expected to share basic materials on their organizations' performance strategies and methods and to answer news media inquiries.

The Baldrige Criteria for Performance Excellence[4]

The Baldrige criteria focus on results and continuous improvement and provide a framework for designing, implementing, and assessing a process for managing all business operations. The Baldrige criteria are used by thousands of organizations of all kinds for self-assessment and training and as a tool to develop performance and business processes. The MBNQA is generally regarded as the most prestigious quality award in the United States, and many states have used the

---

[2] See http://www.nist.gov/public_affairs/factsheet/baldfaqs.html.

[3] See http://www.baldrige.nist.gov/Why_Apply.htm.

[4] This section draws heavily from http://www.quality.nist.gov/PDF_files/2003_Business_Criteria. pdf. Unless otherwise noted, all quotations are taken from this reference.

Baldrige criteria to establish their own quality awards (Przasnyski and Tai, 2002).

The Baldrige criteria are built upon a set of interrelated core values and concepts. Consistent with its emphasis on "continuous improvement," the core concepts and framework are continuously evolving over time. As of 2002, the core values and concepts included visionary leadership; customer-driven excellence; organizational and personal learning; valuing employees and partners; agility; focus on the future; managing for innovation; management by fact; social responsibility; focus on results and creating value; and systems perspective.

These values and concepts provide a foundation for "integrating key requirements within a results-oriented framework that creates a basis for action and feedback," and are embodied in seven criteria that form the basis for organizational self-assessments, for making awards, and for giving feedback to applicants:

Leadership. How senior executives guide the organization and how the organization addresses its responsibilities to the public and practices good citizenship.

Strategic planning. How the organization sets strategic directions and determines key action plans.

Customer and market focus. How the organization determines requirements and expectations of customers and markets.

Information and analysis. How the organization manages, uses, and analyzes data and information to support key organizational processes and the organization's performance management system.

Human resource focus. How the organization enables its workforce to develop its full potential and how the workforce is aligned with the organization's objectives.

Process management. How key production and delivery and support processes are designed, managed, and improved.

Business results. How the organization performs and improves in its key business areas: customer satisfaction, financial and marketplace performance, human resources, supplier and partner performance, and operational performance. The category also examines how the organization performs relative to competitors.

The framework clearly defines the relationship among these criteria as a causal one and emphasizes the central relationship between leadership and business results. It also emphasizes that this relationship is two-sided to indicate the importance of feedback in an effective management system.

Applicants provide information about their efforts in each of the seven areas listed above. The areas are weighted to get a final score and, because of the emphasis on demonstrated performance, the greatest weight is given to organizational performance results (450 out of 1000 points).

Education Criteria for Performance Excellence[5]

In 1999, the Baldrige award program was extended to the education and health sectors. This expansion assumes that the same seven-part framework that underlies the business criteria is adaptable to all organizations, but it recognizes that the guidelines need some adaptation to fit these new sectors. Thus, for education, "customer and market focus" translate into "student, stakeholder, and market focus," "human resource focus" into "faculty and staff focus," and "business results" into "organizational performance results." The underlying belief is that using the same framework for all sectors of the economy fosters cross-sector learning and sharing of information on best practices.

Since 1999, 47 applications have been submitted in the education category.[6] Any for-profit or not-for-profit public or private organization that provides educational services in the United States or its territories is eligible to apply for the award. That includes elementary and secondary schools and school districts; colleges, universities, and

---

[5] This section draws heavily from www.quality.nist.gov/PDF_files/2003_Education_Criteria. pdf. Unless otherwise noted, all quotations are taken from this reference.

[6] It is not clear whether these are 47 distinct educational organizations applying for the award or 47 applications from some smaller number of organizations applying multiple times. Typically, firms apply multiple times before they are successful.

university systems; schools or colleges within a university; professional schools; community colleges; technical schools; and charter schools.

The education criteria are designed to help organizations use an integrated approach to organizational performance management to try to improve education quality in terms of delivery of ever-improving value to students and stakeholders, improvement of overall organizational effectiveness and capabilities, and increased organizational and personal learning.

Four of the education criteria are particularly interesting because they have special relevance to the current accountability systems in education. In particular, the emphases on organizational performance results, strategic planning, information and analysis, and process management fit in well with the current emphases in education on measurable progress against goals; school improvement planning; data-driven decisionmaking; and aligning instruction with standards, goals, and diverse learning styles as characteristics of high-performing schools.

Organizational Performance Results

For education, the Baldrige criterion of excellence in organizational performance translates into "value-added" demonstrated performance, as measured by (1) annual improvement in key measures of performance, especially student learning and (2) demonstrated leadership in performance and performance improvement relative to comparable organizations and/or benchmarks. These measures are similar to what NCLB has required states to establish in terms of adequate yearly progress measures that schools must meet each year—measures that include goals for student achievement and progress, both overall and for groups of students disaggregated by various characteristics (gender, race/ethnicity, English language learners, migrant status, poverty status, and disability status).

However, the Baldrige criteria are broader than those established by NCLB. For example, the organizational performance areas are student learning (150 points); student- and stakeholder-focused results (60 points); budgetary, financial, and market results (60 points); faculty and staff results (60 points); and organizational effectiveness results (60 points). This composite of indicators is intended to ensure that strategies are balanced—that they do not inappropriately make trade-offs among important stakeholders, objectives, or short- and longer-term goals—an important lesson education accountability systems must take into account.

The rationale behind using a "value-added" concept of excellence is that it (1) places the major focus on teaching and learning strategies; (2) poses similar types of challenges for all organizations regardless of resources and incoming students' preparation and abilities; (3) is most likely to stimulate learning-related research and to offer a means to disseminate the results of such research; and (4) offers the potential to create an expanding body of knowledge of successful teaching and learning practices in the widest range of organizations.

Strategic Planning

This criterion examines how the organization develops strategic objectives and action plans, how they are deployed, and how progress is measured. For example, strategy development looks at how the organization prepares for the future, what kinds of projections and options it uses to envision the future, what kinds of data it uses, how it balances short-term and long-term objectives, and how it develops strategies to address key challenges identified in the organizational profile. In addition, organizations are asked to describe how they convert their objectives into action plans, including allocation of resources and measures to track progress, and to project their progress on key performance measures. This is similar to calls for strategic planning as the basis for improving the school. Key to strategic planning is the organization's approach to measurement, analysis, and knowledge management, discussed below.

Information and Analysis

This criterion examines how the organization selects, gathers, and analyzes data and manages and improves its knowledge assets. It echoes calls for principals and teachers to build continuous feedback into their school improvement efforts. A key component of this criterion is gathering comparative data on similar organizations and benchmarks (defined as identifying processes and results that represent best practices and performance for similar organizations). Other key components are making timely, reliable, and accurate information available to staff, students, and stakeholders and sharing best practices among faculty, staff, and stakeholders.

Process Management

Process management refers to the ways in which the organization identifies and manages its key processes for creating student and stakeholder value and maximizing student learning and success. Thus, for example, the organization is asked what the key learning-centered processes that deliver the educational programs are; how the requirements for these processes are determined; how faculty and staff are properly prepared to deliver these processes; how individual differences in student learning rates and styles are accommodated; how new technology is incorporated; how sequencing and linkage among the educational offerings are addressed; how key performance measures are used to control and improve these processes to ensure student success; and how support processes (such as finance, facilities, information services, and human resources) are used to support the learning-centered processes. Obviously, schools' answers to these questions show how they would translate their goals and planning into results.

Evidence on the Baldrige Framework: Effects on Performance

In general, the literature on the Baldrige framework has focused on two questions: (1) To what extent has the causal framework assumed by the Baldrige framework been validated? and (2) Does implementing TQM (which underpins the Baldrige framework) improve operating performance? Obviously, the two are linked—a framework cannot be validated without examining whether it has resulted in the kinds of improvement it promises. However, the approaches taken to answer the two questions appear to use distinctly different methodologies: The first examines the linkages between the various criteria that make up the framework and assesses the direct or indirect causal relationships among them; the second merely uses subsets of firms that either implemented the Baldrige framework or won the Baldrige award and examines whether these firms had better operating performance than comparison groups of firms that did not implement the framework. These two approaches to validity are clearly related; however, because they are so different, we discuss them separately below.

Validating the Framework

Winn and Cameron (1998) administered a 190-item survey data to all permanent noninstructional staff members of a large Midwestern university to investigate the validity of the casual relationships underlying the MBNQA framework, in particular the direct relationship assumed to exist between leadership, system dimensions, and outcomes. Factor analysis revealed that the seven categories were reliable and appropriate. However, confirmatory path analysis did not validate all the relationships in the framework. For example, Winn and Cameron found that, with few exceptions, leaders did not appear to have a direct impact on organizational outcomes. Rather, their influence was felt through the systems and processes they had established. They hypothesize that this may be more typical of higher education than for-profit firms, because of a professionalized workforce and low levels of hierarchical control. They offer the following quality improvement plan for educational institutions: (1) put in place effective leadership committed to change; (2) gather information; (3) use this information to guide strategic planning; (4) based on the strategic plan, design a human resource management system and organizational processes focused on quality. In their model, having effective and efficient organizational processes leads to quality outcomes.

Pannirselvam and Ferguson (2001) used data from the Arizona Governor's Quality Award (which is based on the MBNQA) to study the relationships between the Baldrige categories. Unlike Winn and Cameron (1998), their results confirmed the validity of the Baldrige framework and suggest this might be due to differences in the sample studied and the process used to collect the data. For example, they used data from an actual application process for the quality award that were evaluated by Baldrige examiners, whereas Winn and Cameron (1998) used self-reported rankings from a survey of university personnel. Pannirselvam and Ferguson found that leadership significantly affects all the system constructs (either directly or indirectly) except for strategic quality planning and information management, which was not tested in the model. They also found that customer focus and customer relationship management had the greatest effect on organization performance. They concluded that simply focusing on quality management procedures, without a strong focus on customers, effective leadership, and information management, is not likely to be successful.

Powell (1995) looked at the complementary resources that have to exist for TQM programs to be a success:

> TQM appears to require a culture receptive to change, a motivation to improve, people capable of understanding and implementing TQM's peculiar set of practices, corporate perseverance, leadership qualities such as the capacity to commit, and perhaps some exogenous chance factor that may motivate change and learning. (pp. 21–22)

In a rigorous study of firms that had and had not implemented TQM, Powell concluded that although TQM produces economic value to the firm in the sense of higher financial performance, it does not uniformly do so across all TQM adopters. His empirical research identified three factors as being key to TQM success: executive commitment, open organization, and employee empowerment—all of which create a culture within which TQM can survive. Other TQM staples, such as benchmarking, training, flexible manufacturing, process improvement, and improved measurement, seem to play much smaller roles.

Effect on Operating Performance

The literature addressing this question suffers from a great deal of rhetoric on both sides and, with some exceptions, a lack of objective and empirical evidence. Generally, when one reviews the literature, one must dismiss studies that do not meet the criteria for rigorous research and focus on those that do meet those criteria. Unfortunately, a great deal of attention in the literature is focused on claims and counterclaims made by proponents and opponents. Therefore, we first start with a summary of these claims and counterclaims and then discuss, in more detail, the subset of studies that use rigorous research methods to estimate the impact of TQM on operating performance. By and large, the few studies that offer rigorous empirical evidence suggest that firms implementing TQM do seem to perform better than other firms, although it seems to be important to track performance over the long term rather than to focus simply on short-term results.

For example, the NIST website claims the following:

> Studies by NIST, universities, business organizations, and the U.S. General Accounting Office have found that investing in quality principles and performance excellence pays off in increased productivity, satisfied employees and customers, and improved profitability—both for customers and investors. For example, NIST has tracked a hypothetical stock investment in Baldrige Award winners and applicants receiving site visits. The studies have shown that these companies soundly outperform the Standard and Poor's 500. (http://www.nist.gov/public_affairs/factsheet/baldfaqs.htm)

However, the 1991 General Accounting Office (GAO) study referenced on the NIST website reported that the 20 highest-scoring applicants for the 1988 and 1989 MBNQA had achieved better employee relations, improved product quality, lower costs, and higher customer satisfaction but negligible gains in profitability (U.S. General Accounting Office, 1991—see reference in Powell, 1995, p. 35). But the study did not control for industry factors, did not have a comparison group of non-TQM firms, and did not test for statistical significance of the improvements in performance. Similarly, later studies (reviewed below) showed that the reports regarding the performance of the hypothetical stock investment in Baldrige winners were exaggerated. Opponents, disputing the NIST claims, point to the dismal performance of Cadillac, Federal Express, and Motorola, which suffered declines in market shares and in general profitability levels soon after winning the MBNQA. A study done jointly by Ernst and Young and the American Quality Foundation (1992) suggested that many TQM programs had not been effective and that firms might be wasting millions of dollars on TQM strategies without any improvement in performance. However, this study failed to provide any statistical data on the effectiveness of the TQM programs adopted by these firms.

We turn now to the few rigorous empirical studies. Easton and Jarrell (1998) examined the performance of 108 firms that began implementation of TQM (as operationalized by the Baldrige criteria and judged by carefully structured interviews) between 1981 and 1991 and compared each firm's performance with that of a carefully matched control group that had not implemented TQM. They reported performance changes over a five-year period beginning at the time that firms in their sample started seriously implementing TQM. The major findings of the study were as follows: (a) Long-term performance of firms implementing TQM was better than what it would have been without TQM on both performance measures and stock returns; (b) Firms that had implemented TQM to a greater degree had stronger overall performance; (c) The hypothesis that downsizing that accompanied the implementation of TQM was responsible for the observed positive performance was not supported by the data; and (d) The results were even stronger when the analysis was limited to just manufacturing firms.

Based on a sample of nearly 400 firms that won their first quality award between 1983 and 1993 and several matched control groups, Hendricks and Singhal (1997) found strong evidence that implementing effective TQM (as proxied by winning a quality award) significantly improves operating performance. Firms that won quality awards significantly outperformed control firms on operating income-based measures and on sales growth. There was weak evidence to suggest that award winners were also more successful in controlling costs than comparison firms were, and that they experience higher growth in employment and total assets. These changes in performance were tracked over a ten-year period, from six years before to three years after winning the award.

Przasnyski and Tai (2002), building on earlier work that had shown stock performance of MBNQA winners to be overstated, examined the effect of the MBNQA on the stock performance of recipients from 1988 to 1998 by conducting multiple analyses that adjusted these stock returns for market and industry factors and also annualized them, which the NIST studies had failed to do. They found that the MBNQA winners, properly adjusted for risk and industry, did outperform the S&P 500 but that stocks of matching firms did even better. Indeed, only about half of the MBNQA winners individually did better than the market, but the outstanding performance of a small group of winners boosted the overall group performance. Przasnyski and Tai's evidence suggests that the spectacular returns claimed by earlier studies were largely due to a booming stock market and a booming economy. However, when evaluating the long-term effect of buying and holding stock of these MBNQA firms, they found that those firms outperformed stocks with similar risk.

Sterman, Repenning, and Kofman (1997) explored the unanticipated side effects of a successful quality program in a study of Analog Devices, Inc., a leading manufacturer of integrated circuits. Analog implemented a broad-based TQM program in 1987 that, by all accounts, was highly successful. By 1990, the firm's yield had doubled, manufacturing cycle time had been cut in half, and product defects had fallen by a factor of 10. Yet its share price fell during the same period; return on equity fell to –4 percent; and it experienced its first-ever layoff. The authors point out that several other companies have experienced this same paradox of large improvements in quality not being followed by financial improvement. The authors developed a detailed simulation model using a variety of data and techniques to show that TQM and like improvement programs can present firms with a trade-off between short- and long-run gains. They concluded that while TQM can raise productivity and lower costs in the long run, the companies could well experience excess capacity, financial stress, and pressure for layoffs in the short run—problems that would undermine their commitment to TQM. It needs to be recognized that the link between successful improvement and financial performance is complex and often depends on external factors, such as the economy. A focus on quick results may well be counterproductive. Sterman, Repenning, and Kofman (1997) also warn that different parts of an organization will have different improvement rates and attempting to decompose units/processes may lead to ineffective policies.

This review has offered some evidence that the Baldrige framework appears to be relevant and appropriate for organizations trying to implement quality improvement plans and that implementing TQM principles does appear to offer some promise of successful outcomes. We now turn to the MBNQA Education Criteria and some limited experience of educational institutions with implementing the Baldrige principles.

The K–12 Educational Sector Experience with the MBNQA

As mentioned earlier, the Baldrige award program was extended to the education sector in 1999, and since then there have been two K–12 winners. In addition, the Baldrige framework is being used by several districts and schools in New Jersey, with state sanction, as a means of self-improvement and of meeting the state's assessment criteria.

Winners of the Baldrige Award in Education

In 2001, there were three winners in the Education category: Chugach School District, Alaska; Pearl River School District, New York; and University of Wisconsin-Stout, Wisconsin. Because our primary interest is in the K–12 system, we focus on the first two. The restructuring efforts of the two school districts began long before the MBNQA was established in education—in 1994 and 1991, respectively. We therefore do not know whether their improvement efforts were based on the Baldrige criteria from the beginning or whether they applied for the award when they discovered that their efforts were closely aligned with these criteria. Note that constrained resources did not permit us to examine these cases in detail—we relied on the NIST website for data. Nonetheless, the two districts offer interesting case-studies of how to implement improvement efforts in education.

Chugach School District (CSD), Alaska[7]

CSD consists of 22,000 square miles in south central Alaska and has 214 students, many of whom live in remote areas. CSD was a district in crisis when it began its comprehensive restructuring effort in 1994. In its transformation, CSD applied several of the Baldrige criteria:

Student, Stakeholder, and Market Focus. From the beginning, CSD involved all kinds of stakeholders in its overhaul process: staff, parents, current and past students, school board members, and business and community leaders. Realizing that its students needed more than the regular curriculum provided, the district pioneered a standards-based system of "whole child education" that emphasizes real-life learning situations.

Information and Analysis and Process Management. Instead of credit hours and grade levels, CSD created a continuum of standards for ten content areas that ranged from traditional subject areas and career development skills to cultural awareness and character skills. Students work at their own developmentally appropriate pace, with some graduating as early as age 14 and some at age 21. A student learning profile is developed for each student and updated every three years. Through testing and other means, teachers attempt to determine the individual learning styles of students and tailor learning plans for each student based on this knowledge. Integrated learning and multisensory approaches to teaching are key elements of CSD's approach.

Faculty and Staff Focus. Teachers are offered 30 days of faculty training (double the state average), up to $1,000 for outside training,

---

[7] See http://www.nist.gov/public_affairs/chugach.htm.

a pay-for-performance system that rewards individual and district-wide accomplishments, and flexible working conditions that allow for sharing or rotating jobs.

Organizational Performance Results. Faculty turnover, which averaged 55 percent between 1975 and 1994, has fallen to 12 percent. Students are meeting standards that are higher than those set by the state.

Pearl River School District (PRSD), New York[8]

PRSD is located 20 miles north of New York City in Rockland County and encompasses 2,500 K–12 students and 1,000 adults to whom it provides continuing education. It has 203 teachers distributed among three elementary schools, one middle school, and one high school. Its transformation also rests on a systematic application of the Baldrige seven-part framework.

Strategic Planning. Since 1991, the district has focused on three goals: improving academic performance, improving public perception of the district by implementing quality principles and values, and maintaining fiscal stability and improving efficiency. PRSD has created a team structure that makes the success of students a shared responsibility transcending grade levels and schools.

Student, Stakeholder, and Market Focus. Like CSD, PRSD involved all its stakeholders in its transformation.

Information and Analysis and Process Management. PRSD maintains a "balanced scorecard," a scannable composite of indicators of progress in meeting goals and objectives that allows continuous tracking of district performance.[9] Finer-grained tracking measures are also maintained at the school, grade, classroom, teacher, and student levels. Curriculum mapping uses a five-step approach (analyze, align, act, assess, and standardize); these maps detail the content areas cov-

---

[8] See http://www.nist.gov/public_affairs/peralriver.htm [sic].

[9] The balanced scorecard was developed outside of the Baldrige framework. Recall, however, that the Baldrige criteria are prescriptive not with respect to methods or tools but with respect to an underlying philosophy. Organizations have a lot of leeway to develop and implement approaches that best fit their needs.

ered, the method of instruction, and the assessment techniques used. The maps are adjusted quarterly, guided by data analyses. High-need students are tracked closely by the special child study team in each school. When performance goals are met by all students, instructional strategies and curriculum design are standardized. Both formal and informal evaluation processes measure teachers' performance against the district's goals and objectives.

Organizational Performance Results. Over the past eight years, spending for instruction has risen by 43 percent, largely due to savings from operational efficiencies. The percentage of students graduating with a Regent's diploma has increased from 60 percent in 1996 to 86 percent in 2001, and the percentage of students scoring "3" or better on Advanced Placement courses has risen by 53 percentage points over the past five years. In addition, 75 percent of special education students take the SAT I exam, compared with 3 percent statewide and 2 percent nationwide. Student and parent satisfaction are at all-time highs, as is the satisfaction of staff and faculty.

Other Users of the Baldrige Criteria

Many education organizations that are not formally applying for the Baldrige award nonetheless use the Baldrige criteria for assessment and improvement. The most widespread example of the use of the Baldrige criteria for excellence is in New Jersey, where the New Jersey Department of Education permits school systems to use the New Jersey Quality Achievement Award criteria—based on the Baldrige award criteria—as an alternative to its state assessment criteria. This came about as a result of the larger efforts in the state to advance excellence on all fronts. In 1989, a nonprofit organization, Quality New Jersey (QNJ), was founded with the ambitious mission of advancing the state of excellence in New Jersey. Quality Education New Jersey (QENJ) is a focus Group of QNJ with a mission to advance excellence in education through continuous improvement, based on the Baldrige model.

QENJ offers training, tools, and assistance to schools and school districts that wish to transform themselves using the Baldrige criteria and provides coaching and mentoring throughout the process. In

January 2001, QENJ formed a consortium of the schools and part-ners that were then participating in the Baldrige model process and volunteered to share their experiences. The mission of the consortium is to take the lead in bringing together educational, business, and governmental partners for the purpose of continuously improving school and district organizational performance and student achieve-ment. Thus far, 14 school districts have joined the consortium.

Implications for Education

There are important lessons to be learned from MBNQA for educa-tional accountability. The education criteria provide guidelines on conducting an institutional self-assessment based on a detailed orga-nizational profile and developing a strategic plan linked to clearly identified goals and reinforced by an information and analysis system to collect data and monitor progress toward those goals. Regardless of whether institutions adopt the full Baldrige framework, an institu-tional self-assessment may be inherently beneficial. In addition, the education criteria are designed to help schools and school districts use an integrated approach to organizational performance management with a view to enhancing overall organizational effectiveness and ca-pabilities and improving learning among students, faculty, and the organization itself. Chugach and Pearl River School Districts and New Jersey schools and districts offer prime examples of how to adapt these business core values and concepts to education and use them as the basis for self-assessment and improvement. Thus, the Baldrige framework can help support broader accountability efforts. However, educators may find it difficult to translate business criteria or to see their applicability without technical assistance.

Institutional Self-Assessment May Be Inherently Beneficial

Institutional self-assessment and improvement are by themselves a type of accountability. When an institution, be it a school or a school district, undertakes this type of focused examination, it is holding it-self accountable for achieving its mission. The fact that some educational institutions are applying for the Baldrige award may be a sign that they are serious about their professional responsibilities—even without the impetus from an external accountability system.[10] Whether or not schools or districts actually apply is immaterial—going through the process itself could be invaluable. And, if the feedback is indeed as useful as the comments would indicate, the investment of $500 for the application may be a small price to pay for having a Baldrige examiner review the organization, its processes, and its strategic planning and provide constructive feedback.

The Baldrige Process Supports Accountability

The Baldrige approach can also be effective as an institutional improvement strategy embedded in a larger accountability system. In particular, the Baldrige approach might work well in the context of NCLB. States are required to identify schools (and districts) that fail to make adequate progress in meeting standards for two consecutive years as "in need of improvement." These schools and districts will be required to develop or revise their plans to address identified needs, and they are to be provided technical assistance by the states and districts through school support teams and other support mechanisms. If schools identified for improvement fail to show progress for two full years, states and districts can take further corrective actions, as described earlier in Chapter One.

   For the NCLB approach to be successful, districts and states must have the capacity and the knowledge to help schools improve and schools, given this assistance, must have the capacity to improve. There is evidence that this capacity is not widespread. As Hamman and Schenck (2002) point out, "if districts have not been able to assist schools in need of improvement, there is little chance they will be able to turn around low-performing schools by taking corrective action, unless some action is taken to boost the capacity for reform at the district level" (p. 3). Even if districts knew how to improve

---

[10] Of course, some institutions may be motivated by the external credibility conferred by winning the MBNQA, which could bring greater funding and a greater ability to attract higher-quality teachers and students.

schools, district support by itself is not enough to change a school. Schools need to have the capacity to reform. Researchers have suggested five components that are key to school improvement: teachers' knowledge, skills, and dispositions; professional community; program coherence; technical resources; and principal leadership (Newmann et al., 2000). Moreover, schools need to have a strategy for improvement. The U.S. Department of Education (2001) indicates that school reform must be a four-step process: needs assessment and goal setting; careful planning and choice of a set of coherent strategies to best fit identified needs and priorities; focused, sustained implementation; and evaluation and feedback to facilitate continuous improvement. Unfortunately, many of the low-performing schools and districts have little idea of how to carry out these four steps or how to approach this process systematically.

This is where the Baldrige criteria and framework could play an important role. Developing a detailed organizational profile is the first step in the Baldrige process. The discipline imposed by having to set forth clearly the environment in which the organization operates; the organization's culture (purpose, mission, vision, and goals); its structure and governance system; its key stakeholders; the regulatory environment; key partner relationships; and the major technologies, equipment, and facilities available could be very useful to a failing school. The guidance the Baldrige criteria offer for bringing together processes, resources (broadly defined), and data to serve strategic goals may offer schools and districts struggling to meet the demands of NCLB a systematic and strategic approach to continuous improvement.

Educators May Find It Difficult to Understand and Translate the Criteria

A key assumption underlying the previous section was that school principals and teachers have the time, the resources, the interest, and the capacity to undertake a self-assessment based on the Baldrige criteria—which may be a large assumption in the case of failing schools. Schools might also be confused about what the criteria mean and how to apply them in a particular context. For example, schools might have trouble defining short-term and long-term objectives, identifying key challenges, and articulating how best to deploy resources to address these challenges. In some instances, they may not know how to develop and implement a strong assessment strategy or how to use data for continuous feedback and improvement. In addition, educational institutions have traditionally resisted being compared to business organizations and being asked to learn lessons from the business sector.

It is likely that schools and districts will need help in getting over this initial reluctance and lack of experience in thinking about their organizations strategically and in a business context. States and business organizations could be very useful in providing information and technical assistance, offering how-to workshops, and partnering schools with businesses, as New Jersey has done. For example, it might be helpful to call a meeting at which the two winners of the Baldrige award talk about the details of how they applied the criteria and the challenges they faced, along with the successes they achieved. States could help by endorsing such dissemination activity, giving it greater publicity, and providing time and money for attendance. If schools and districts get over the initial hurdles, the seven-part framework put forward by the Baldrige program could help lay the foundations for transformation.

Some Caveats

It is important to stress that even if schools and districts go through the Baldrige process, change may be difficult. To implement the needed reforms, schools may require much more flexibility and autonomy than currently exists in the educational sector, given the highly unionized labor force and regulations governing curriculum, instructional time, etc. So, unless the process is supported by structural changes, there is no guarantee of success. Second, we saw earlier that, while the Baldrige process and other TQM approaches support long-term goals, unanticipated side effects may well end up undermining the effort in the short run. Education, especially under NCLB, is driven to demand immediate success; promising innovations have often been abandoned before they have had a chance to prove themselves. This may well happen with such approaches as MBNQA and other TQM efforts. Third, it is important to be aware of the self-selection bias that may be present in the findings presented here in support of the Baldrige process. Organizations that use the criteria and fail to improve are not likely to apply for the award, so examining winners and their performance is biased in favor of finding positive outcomes. Nonetheless, we believe that the integrated, systematic approach offered by the Baldrige process may prove useful in helping schools understand what is needed for improvement.

CHAPTER THREE

Toyota Production System/Lean Manufacturing

Heather Barney and Sheila Nataraj Kirby

The Toyota Production System (TPS) is the unique manufacturing system pioneered by Eiji Toyoda and Taiichi Ohno at the Toyota Motor Company in Japan after World War II. Although it was created as an automotive production system, it is now widely recognized for its revolutionary approach to doing business, which provides more choice to consumers, more decisionmaking involvement for workers, and greater, more efficient productivity to companies. TPS is synonymous with "lean production" or "lean manufacturing," a term coined by researchers in the International Motor Vehicle Program at the Massachusetts Institute of Technology (MIT) (Womack, Jones, and Roos, 1990). The school-as-production-unit analogy (Finn, 2002) suggests that there may be benefits in examining TPS or lean manufacturing from an educational perspective.

As in the previous chapter, we first outline the characteristics of this system, examine the evidence about how well the principles underlying the system have worked in practice, and finally discuss their potential application to education.[1]

Overview of TPS/Lean Manufacturing

TPS is the set of operational principles created by Toyota, a recognized leader in quality automobile manufacturing. Many American

---

[1] See Cook and Graser (2001) for a succinct history of the genesis of lean manufacturing.

companies, in both auto manufacturing and diverse other fields, have attempted to imitate TPS best practices or lean manufacturing. A joint General Motors and Toyota effort to import TPS to the United States resulted in the transformation of GM's Fremont, California, plant—one of the worst in the country in terms of quality, productivity and morale—into the New United Motor Manufacturing plant, which was recognized within five years as one of the best (Adler, 1993).

Babson (1995) offers a summary of some of the characteristics of lean production:

> Inventories in a "lean" plant are taken on a just-in-time basis to minimize handling and expose defective parts before they accumulate in the warehouse; stockpiles of in-process work are also sharply reduced so that defects are immediately exposed at their source, before they fill the plant's repair bays with defective products; "indirect" labor (supervision, inspection, and maintenance) is pared and specialized job classifications are reduced or eliminated, replaced by teams of cross-trained production workers who rotate jobs and take on responsibilities for quality control, repair, housekeeping, and preventive maintenance. (p. 6)

Liker (1998) points out, following Womack and Jones (1996), that lean manufacturing can be described in terms of three essential elements:

- Making the product flow through the system without interruption and wasted time
- A culture in which everyone is dedicated to continuous improvement
- A "pull" system that ensures that production is tied closely to demand, so no products are built until there is demand for them, and inputs are supplied at the appropriate time.

These elements translate into several principles that characterize lean manufacturing. Three of them—a focus on the value stream, standardization of jobs, and worker empowerment—are important for our purposes because they offer some implications for improving educational accountability.

Focus on the Value Stream

Lean manufacturing requires manufacturers to understand every step in the process—*the value stream*—to ensure efficient production. This requires that there be no unnecessary steps or waste in the process (Cook and Graser, 2001). In other words, every supplier who is connected to the flow path is necessary to production, and no suppliers who are necessary to production have been left out of the flow path (Spear and Bowen, 1999). The design of such pathways, for both the automobiles being manufactured and for service goods like managerial support, customer service, and so on, requires careful consideration of the value provided by each supplier along the path, the end-value that is expected from the pathway and the elements that create that sum total of value. Processes and TPS may be envisioned as streams in which value flows from the initial supplier, growing larger through the input of each successive supplier along the pathway until it reaches its final destination with the customer, much as water in an actual stream flows from small headwaters to a final destination in an ocean or lake, gaining strength from the tributaries that feed in along the way.

Paying attention to the value stream of production in TPS creates several important advantages. First, instilling in workers and managers a broad understanding of the process, the desired end-point, and the role of each particular job along the way helps to foster the concept of *jidoka*, which basically means "don't pass along problems to others," and encourages workers and managers to feel responsible not only for their particular task but also for the final product. In addition, the focus on stream and flows removes the "black box" between inputs and outputs and so allows problems to easily be traced to their root causes and dealt with appropriately. Finally, issues of product quality can be dealt with immediately and effectively because attention to the pathways of production allows quality control to be built into processes rather than "inspected in" at the end. Instead of waiting for a car to roll off the assembly line before worrying about how well it was made, TPS creates more-effective quality control because each worker along the assembly line knows what steps contribute to the final product and checks that the steps are done correctly as they are completed.

Standardization

Eliminating waste and making value flow through the system requires that "all work shall be highly specified as to content, sequence, timing, and outcome" (Spear and Bowen, 1999, p. 98). Workers perform jobs that are intricately scripted, down to the order in which they tighten bolts and how much time each bolt should take. All processes and actions in the plant are similarly specified and standardized: A part moves rigidly from a particular machine to another through the assembly line, even if an alternate machine that could accomplish the same task is available first; a worker always receives assistance from the same manager, even if another is nearby or more immediately prepared to deal with the problem. Variation and "chance" are minimized as much as possible in all activities.

Demanding rigid standardization in all aspects of production makes it easy for workers and managers alike to immediately identify problems, since any deviation from the standard represents something awry. More important, though, standardization in TPS is seen as the "essential precondition for learning" (Adler, 1993), and is thus regarded as the key to continuous improvement, system learning, and organizational improvement. Standardized work allows Toyota workers to become scientists investigating their own work, using hypothesis-testing and the scientific method to learn about and improve their jobs.

Toyota workers use the scientific method to improve their jobs in the following manner. When a job is designed, both a particular process and a particular outcome are specified. The expected outcome rests on two hypotheses: that the job can in fact be performed by the worker in the manner specified and that, if performed as specified, the job does lead to the anticipated outcome. With every repetition of this standardized job that is subsequently performed, the worker is implicitly carrying out a controlled experiment to test those hypotheses and to either confirm or refute them (Spear and Bowen, 1999). Equipped with the knowledge gained through these experiments that, for example, the job doesn't work as intended or that the worker doesn't have the skills to perform as required, workers and managers can then remedy the problems identified through their experiments. If variation were allowed in the way the work is performed, however, it would be difficult to determine where the problem lies, or even if there is a problem at all. Standardization creates the conditions necessary for controlled scientific inquiry and hypothesis-testing, which enable workers to learn the intricate details of every job, whether the job is effective, and why.

Worker Empowerment

Empowering workers by treating them as professionals is an important principle underlying lean manufacturing. According to Womack, Jones, and Roos (1990), the lean production system

> provides workers with the skills they need to control their work environment and the continuing challenge of making the work go more smoothly . . . This creative tension involved in solving complex problems is precisely what has separated manual factory work from professional "think" work in the age of mass production. (pp. 101–102)

Adler (1993) further elaborates:

> Formal work standards developed by industrial engineers and imposed on workers are alienating. But procedures that are designed by workers themselves in a continuous, successful effort to improve productivity, quality, skills, and understanding can humanize even the most disciplined forms of bureaucracy. (p. 98)

Thus, information gleaned from standardization and hypothesis-testing is not sent off to a team of industrial engineers who redesign jobs or pathways using theoretical models and then impose their design on workers. Rather, the workers use their own knowledge of their work to design and implement improvements for the plant, assisted by managers who act as teachers and resource guides. Workers are trained in problem-solving and work analysis techniques and given responsibility for identifying problems and then designing improvements and solutions using the scientific method (Adler, 1993, p. 103). The management hierarchy in TPS serves as a source of support and expertise rather than command and control.

Empowering workers in this way has a number of important advantages in TPS. It ensures that all jobs are designed by the people who are most familiar with them, so specific knowledge is fully utilized and worker buy-in is enhanced. It increases workers' motivation and interest in their own improvement. In addition, a system that grants local authority for problem-solving allows solutions to be found quickly while problems are still small and localized, with minimal loss of needed information.

Evidence for Effects of TPS/Lean Manufacturing on Production and Workers

The literature on lean manufacturing is enormous, and we cannot hope to do justice to it here. This section, therefore, presents a few selected findings that show both sides of the picture in terms of effects on production and empowerment or exploitation of workers. By and large, the case studies of various firms point to the huge dividends that investment in lean production can bring in terms of improved productivity, quality, and lower costs. For example:

- The MIT assembly plant study revealed that implementing lean production methods led to an eight-hour advantage in labor-hours per car and a 50 percent reduction in number of assembly defects per 100 cars in lean automobile plants compared with traditional mass production methods (Womack, Jones, and Roos, 1990).
- Plant No. 6 of Delphi Saginaw Steering Systems reduced its number of customer rejects from 2,000 parts per million in

1993 to 75 parts per million in 1997 and costs by 6–11 percent almost every year (Woolson and Husar, 1998).
- Freudenberg-NOK, the world's largest manufacturer of sealing components, saw dramatic improvements in quality, delivery times, and cost reductions, and a growth in sales from $200 million to $600 million in four years, with unprecedented profit levels (Day, 1998).
- Pall Gelman Sciences, a maker of medical products, cut inventory by almost two-thirds and lead times by half, at the same time improving productivity and quality significantly (Zayko, Hancock, and Broughman, 1998).

However, Choi (1998), in discussing the efforts of seven small automotive parts suppliers to implement continuous improvement (CI), shows that only three had any degree of success. He identifies several pitfalls for small- to medium-size companies when implementing lean production:

- **Alienation of line leaders.** Line leaders who were given the responsibility of meeting both production goals and improvement goals felt a deep sense of conflict between trying to decide whether to allow the workers to work on improvements or on production activities. This juggling act became even tougher when the company fell behind in its production. At that time, improvement took a back seat to production and workers were prevented from going to their CI meetings.
- **Treating CI simply as a problem-solving activity or as something to do when there was a spare moment.** In one company, workers could not distinguish the CI program from other more isolated and disjointed problem-solving activities. CI must involve a large body of workers and entail a more concerted approach. Often, CI activities became simply "fire-fighting." The improvement efforts in another company also became intermittent because of a preoccupation with meeting delivery deadlines. At that company, CI was treated as something to do when people were not preoccupied with daily production.

- **Viewing CI as a management program or a worker program.** To get buy-in from the managers, one company appointed them to lead the CI committees rather than the line workers who were initially more enthusiastic. As a result, the CI program was seen as a management program. In another company, which viewed the CI program largely as a "worker thing," workers' efforts were overseen by a group consisting of managers. This group also reviewed all proposals from the line leaders for improvement, slowing the process and causing workers to react negatively.

Worker Empowerment or Worker Exploitation?

Lean production proponents claim that the system solves "the labor problem" and replaces the traditional adversarial relationship between workers and management with mutual problem-solving. Womack, Jones, and Roos (1990) acknowledge that lean production depends strongly on the requirement that workers work very hard and be very committed to the process. For example, Babson (1995, p. 16) describes the many roles that workers in TPS plants must play:

> Asked to perform the same direct-labor tasks that characterize mass production, the worker in a lean plant must also continuously improve the process, rotate through jobs, and do such indirect tasks as inspection, repair, and minor maintenance.

There is a great deal of controversy over whether lean production works the way it is supposed to in terms of worker empowerment. Eaton (1995) surveyed managers and union representatives in a large sample of manufacturing firms in 1990 and concluded that lean production is neither inherently exploitative nor empowering and suggests that a proactive union can help defend workers' well-being in these systems. However, Parker and Slaughter (1995) describe several examples of lean production in practice and suggest that lean production is better described as "management by stress." They conclude that authority and real power move upward whereas accountability is forced down to lower levels, at the expense of workers' long-term interests, health, and safety. A 1992 survey by the Confederation of Japanese Automobile Workers' Unions of 6,000 of its members grimly concluded that its workers were feeling "petered out" and that "under the pretext of sharing a common destiny . . . companies do seem to have been too demanding of their workers" (cited in Babson, 1995, p. 17). Similarly, in a detailed study of CAMI—a joint venture of General Motors and Suzuki widely regarded as a lean production showcase—Rinehart, Huxley, and Robertson (1997) found that lean production translated into lean staffing, a penchant to load more and more work onto jobs, and a lot of overtime, which led to a surprise worker strike against CAMI in 1992. Cook (1996), in her book review of Babson's edited volume, *Lean Work,* offers a useful summary of this literature:

> The overriding message of Lean Work is that the idea that the lean production system necessarily leads to fulfilled and empowered factory workers should be reexamined. The lean system may be extremely efficient, offering higher profits and competitive advantages . . . Managers, however, should not confuse their appreciation of the cost savings and other benefits of the lean production system with worker gratification at making these improvements possible. (p. 336)

Applying TPS/Lean Manufacturing to Education

Applying the principles of TPS/lean manufacturing to accountability and organizational improvement in education means translating the firm and assembly line production model into the context of schools and educators. Although it is not a perfect analogy, there is a natural overlay of the manufacturing model in the educational context. In education, the final product is not cars, but rather the learning of students over the course of their K–12 careers. The workers who perform the direct work of "manufacturing" this product are classroom teachers, and classroom instruction and curriculum are the jobs and processes along the "assembly line." The plant managers, overseeing the assembly line work, are principals, superintendents, and other administrators and policymakers involved in the educational system. Customers with the greatest interest in the final product include parents, the students themselves, and other stakeholders such as business and political leaders.

Of course, the analogy between manufacturing and education is imperfect, and there are some important differences. First, the TPS process relies on consistency in starting materials. In contrast, education strives to produce proficiency on the same standards from very different student "starting materials."[2]

The second difference between the manufacturing and educational sectors relates to the organization of production. Toyota's organizational structure involves—at least in theory—small, close-knit work teams that focus on a handful of tasks that are repeated frequently in the manufacturing process, therefore allowing for quick iterations of problem-solving and improvement techniques. Generally, in education (particularly in elementary schools), teachers tend to be relatively isolated in their classrooms, responsible for a myriad of tasks and instructional units, many of which do not recur. Finally, the analogy likens teaching and learning to assembling parts, which is an oversimplified view of the instructional process. To some extent, teachers are attempting to fit pieces together in a sequential manner to create a complex whole, but most educators would disagree with this description of the learning process. Yet, despite these differences, the "school as firm" analogy remains quite popular in the accountability literature, and it seems worthwhile to draw out its implications.

---

[2] Of course, there is differentiation in educational outcomes, particularly at the secondary level. Yet the rhetoric of NCLB nevertheless emphasizes the attainment of common standards.

Implications for Education

Greater Focus on Value Streams Could Improve Educational Outcomes

For education, the TPS/lean production focus on value stream points out the vital importance of looking at the entire process of creating value, not merely focusing on such inputs as expenditures on various categories—as is done in bureaucratic accountability, or outputs—as is the case with standards-based assessments. Teachers and administrators would need to address an extended sequence of questions: What final outcomes are desired? What intermediate steps add value that contributes to those outcomes? When in the "production line" should each piece of intermediate value be added? Which pieces build on other pieces? What necessary value might currently be missing from the curriculum and instructional process? What steps in the current process do not add value toward the desired outcome? For example, if a school wanted to raise student achievement in mathematics, staff would have to determine which mathematical skills and processes students are currently learning, what additional skills are potentially attainable, where in the curriculum those skills are most effectively taught, which parts of the curriculum can be sacrificed to make room for the new material, what sequence of activities will promote mastery of those skills and procedures, how instruction will be differentiated based on student differences, where those activities can be added to the existing sequence of lessons, and how teachers would know whether the skills have been imparted or not.

Jidoka also seems equally as appropriate for education as it is for manufacturing. It suggests that educators put more energy into identifying and dealing with problems immediately and at their source. The goal of TPS is to build in quality rather than to fix the product after it is completed. Thus, in the process of educating a student, frequent assessments would allow teachers to diagnose a lack of student knowledge or understanding on a particular subject. This situation could be addressed immediately, both to fill the gap before the student is sent on to other lessons that may well build on earlier foundations and to identify the root problem with the way the lesson was taught in the first place. Such a process would allow instruction and curriculum on that topic to be improved for future cohorts of students.

In practical terms, a focus on value stream in education might mean creating accountability measures that take into account not only test scores and other outcome measures but also process indicators dealing with curriculum, teaching practice, and so on. Another possibility might be more-frequent classroom-based assessments that could trigger supplemental instruction for students and guidance for future improvement on the tested lesson for teachers if students did not show adequate mastery. Greater communication and coordination across grade levels within a school and between secondary schools and their feeder elementary schools would also create a stronger sense of the flow of value from kindergarten through to a student's high school graduation. Finally, the concept of *jidoka* and an eye on students' education as a whole would likely dictate an end to social promotion for those who had not built an adequate foundation in one grade for success in the next.

Creating a greater value-stream focus in education could be challenging. For example, process indicators that are valid, reliable, and meaningful can be quite difficult and costly to devise and collect, so developers of any new accountability measures must take into account the potential burden on schools and teachers. Frequent testing can help monitor students and the value they are gaining as they pass through pathways of instruction, but current testing regimes are sometimes criticized for already taking away too much instructional time. It would therefore be important to ensure that additional assessments enhance rather than detract from instruction. Retaining students in grade has been a popular proposal for some time, but it can be politically divisive, and research on the net effects of its learning benefits as opposed to potential losses in terms of children's social growth has not yet ended the debate. Implementation of value-stream-oriented programs would need to be slow and deliberate to account for these potential pitfalls.

Teaching Practices May Benefit from Standardization

The emphasis on hypothesis-testing and continuous improvement that is fostered in TPS/lean production through the first rule of standardization is an equally important goal in education accountability. If implemented in a TPS-style framework, standardized work and implicit hypothesis-testing might help create the kind of reflective, responsive teaching practices that education reformers want. With its links to the scientific method and controlled experiments, TPS-style standardization seems well aligned with NCLB's call for "scientifically based practice."

In practical terms, TPS suggests that classroom teachers could use standardized instruction and curriculum and, by paying attention to both actual outcomes and expected outcomes, engage in the same sort of hypothesis-testing that Toyota workers engage in. For example, if teaching phonics using methods from Reading Recovery for 30 minutes a day is expected to result in a given level of reading proficiency after four weeks but does not, the problem should lie with either the teacher's ability to provide the instruction as specified or with the instruction itself. The problem can be corrected by retraining the teacher or improving the lesson plans. Without such standardization and implicit hypothesis-testing, however, it is far more difficult to locate the source of the problem when students are not reading proficiently.

It is possible to carry such standardization too far, though. Excessively scripted classroom practice could be detrimental because it might fail to recognize the unique instructional needs of different students and the unique instructional strengths of different teachers. The educational implications of standardization would have to be carefully weighed against the potential benefits. For example, no amount of standardization of practice can eliminate the heterogeneity of the students in the instructional process. And large amounts of standardization are likely to have negative effects on teachers' morale and sense of professionalism. Minimizing chance and variation is far more difficult in education than in manufacturing, although it could be possible to reduce variation in some aspects of classroom instruction and curriculum.

Other applications of the TPS/lean production concept of standardization and the emphasis on system learning might suggest reforms on a macro level to enhance educational research. National standardized testing, for example, would allow for better comparisons across classrooms, schools, districts, and states. Extending standardized curriculum and instruction from the school level to the district, state, or national level would narrow the sources of variation in the educational process even further, and so could reveal even more interesting and significant relationships between what students know and are able to do and the influence of teachers, classroom, school, family, and community on learning.

Worker Empowerment Could Improve Educational Practices

From TPS/lean production, educators can learn the importance of empowering teachers by training them to problem-solve and then expecting them to be self-reflective and to continuously improve their practice. The production of a child's education across multiple teachers and a lengthy timetable is even more complex than the manufacture of an automobile, and the success of TPS/lean production suggests that centralized control may not be the answer. Toyota engineers cannot micro-manage every aspect of the assembly line, just as it would be impossible for policymakers and administrators to oversee the minute details of classroom instruction across an entire school or district. In the same way that Toyota benefits from delegating the responsibility of individual job design to assembly line workers, education might benefit from assigning greater responsibility to teachers. Although policymakers and researchers certainly have expertise in a number of areas to lend to the task, they often cannot understand the realities of the teaching experience as well as teachers can.

For the "managers" in the educational system, TPS suggests that—by fostering the advantageous combination of teachers' specific knowledge with the higher-level expertise and guiding resources provided by researchers, administrators, and policymakers—principals, superintendents, and others could offer support rather than control, thus enhancing the process of continuous improvement. For school, district, state, and national education administrators, empowering

teachers requires an emphasis on providing better support and training at all levels rather than excessive control or financial rewards and
sanctions that may encourage quick results but bring about less-
effective system improvement.

Previously, we saw that workers can become overwhelmed by
increasing levels of responsibility and that lean production can turn
into "management by stress." It would also be important to guard
against this situation in education, where teachers already labor under
tremendous workloads, conflicting mandates, and students with
varying abilities. To be truly "empowered," teachers need to be provided with time, resources, and training.

TPS/Lean Production Must Be Used as a Complete System

Finally, it is vital for policymakers and administrators to understand
that the elements of TPS/lean production cannot be implemented
piecemeal. Standardization of work that is imposed from the top of
the organizational system rather than bubbling up from the bottom
alienates teachers and is merely another application of bureaucratic
accountability rather than a novel new solution. Merely empowering
teachers without the logical, scientific, ordering of thought provided
through standardization and hypothesis-testing is not a new system
but is rather the embodiment of inanity that critics like Finn (2002)
see in professional accountability. A focus on value streams without
either the feedback of standardization or the ground-level expertise of
teachers would create an organizational systems problem of huge pro-
portions that would prove nearly impossible to solve. The key to the
success of TPS/lean production is the dynamic interaction of all three
of these principles, leading to a coherent organization-wide system in
which problems are dealt with at their source, on the lowest level possible, and with continuous and immediate objective feedback.

Closely Translating TPS Practices to Education Is Challenging

The TPS/lean production analogy presents some difficulties for educators. First, the empowerment of teachers may prove politically difficult, since additional authority for educators is sometimes perceived
to be disempowering for communities and parents. In addition, the

system requires teachers to possess a strong understanding of prob-lem-solving techniques and scientific experimentation, which would necessitate substantial investment in new training. This is not a fatal flaw, but policymakers must recognize the time and resources needed and offer appropriate support.

Another fundamental conflict between standardization and worker empowerment in education relates to curriculum. One way that schools are standardizing instruction is by adopting highly scripted curriculum materials. This scripted approach may narrow teachers' focus to the extent that they are unable or unwilling to thoughtfully examine their own practice.

Finally, and perhaps most fundamentally, the important organi-zational differences between an auto manufacturing plant and a na-tionwide educational system discussed previously suggest some vital preconditions for the TPS system to be successful. The dispersed or-ganizational structure of the education system creates an enormous need for an effective communications infrastructure that could link teachers into larger communities and facilitate continuous sharing and analysis of aggregated data and experiences, as well as wide dis-semination of improvements in instructional methods and curricu-lum design. Some education reformers have long advocated such teacher learning communities, and effective continuous improvement would require their implementation at multiple levels, from the school to the district, state, nation, and perhaps the world.

CHAPTER FOUR

The Job Training Partnership Act and the Workforce Investment Act

Sheila Nataraj Kirby

The Job Training Partnership Act (JTPA) was passed by the U.S. Congress in 1982 to provide job training and services to those facing serious barriers to employment. The JTPA program was unique at the time because it linked explicit performance standards with performance incentives. In 1998, it was succeeded by the Workforce Investment Act (WIA), which was intended to provide greater accountability through its use of new performance measures. The JTPA and WIA provide a useful illustration of what happens when institutional performance is rewarded according to specific, explicit outcome measures. Thus, the JTPA and WIA lessons are relevant to any discussion of educational accountability that involves establishing specific outcome targets. In this chapter, we describe the basic characteristics of the JTPA and WIA, discuss how the programs worked in practice, and draw out their implications for educational accountability.

Overview of the Job Training Partnership Act

Congress passed the Job Training Partnership Act in 1982 to provide job training and other services for youth and adults who face serious barriers to employment. This training and assistance was supposed to result in increased employment and earnings, increased educational and occupational skills, and decreased welfare dependency (Sec. 2, http://www.doleta.gov/regs/statutes/jtpalaw.asp). The program operated through local training centers often called service delivery areas (SDAs) that were given a local monopoly on providing JTPA-funded services. JTPA was a voluntary program designed to serve unemployed individuals who met the income eligibility limits or had a low family income in the six months preceding application to the program. Two key features of JTPA were the use of performance standards and performance incentives.

Performance Standards

The act stated:

> The Congress recognizes that job training is an investment in human capital and not an expense. In order to determine whether that investment has been productive, the Congress finds that (1) it is essential that criteria for measuring the return on this investment be developed; and (2) the basic return on the investment is to be measured by long-term economic self-sufficiency, increased employment and earnings, reductions in welfare dependency, and increased educational attainment and occupational skills. (Sec. 106 (a), http://www.doleta.gov/regs/statutes/jtpalaw.asp)

The Department of Labor (DOL) was charged with developing a workable set of performance measures. For adults, these included placement in unsubsidized employment; retention for not less than six months in unsubsidized employment; an increase in earnings, including hourly wages; a reduction in welfare dependency; and the acquisition of skills, including basic skills, required to promote continued employability in the local labor market or the acquisition of a high school diploma or the equivalent of the diploma, if the acquisition of such skills or diploma is in addition to obtaining one or more of the other outcomes. For youth, these measures included attainment of employment competencies; dropout prevention and recovery; secondary and postsecondary school completion or the equivalent of such completion; and enrollment in other training programs, apprenticeships, or postsecondary education, or enlistment in the

Armed Forces (Sec. 106 (b), http://www.doleta.gov/regs/statutes/jtpalaw.asp).

Each program year, the federal government defined target levels for each core outcome measure (employment rates either at termination from JTPA or 13 weeks after, and average wage rates among participants who were employed, computed both for all participants and those on welfare) and provided a regression model that states could use to adjust the targets for differences in economic conditions and participant characteristics among centers (Heckman, Heinrich, and Smith, forthcoming). This is very similar to what is done in health care, which uses risk adjustment models to correct for patient characteristics before judging the quality or effectiveness of medical care (see Chapter Seven).

Individual states could adopt these federal standards or modify/augment them within broad limits. Many states added additional measures that provided incentives targeted at services for particular groups within the JTPA-eligible population. JTPA became a prototype for other government programs and led to the passage of the Government Performance and Results Act of 1993 (GPRA), which required each federal agency to establish performance goals.[1]

Performance Incentives

JTPA also provided financial incentives if the performance of SDAs exceeded the set standards. States were given considerable latitude in setting the "award function," the rule that determined the payoff to SDAs as a function of their performance relative to the standards or to each other. Although states varied a great deal in the weight they assigned different measures, the one common feature was that the

---

[1] Under GPRA, the head of each agency was required to submit an annual performance plan that established performance goals to define the level of performance to be achieved by a program activity; expressed those goals in an objective, quantifiable, and measurable form; established performance indicators to be used in measuring or assessing the relevant outputs, service levels, and outcomes of each program activity; provided a basis for comparing actual program results with the established performance goals; and described the means to be used to verify and validate measured values (Sec. 2, 3, 4: http://www.whitehouse.gov/omb/mgmt-gpra/gplaw2m.html).

greatest weight was given to employment and wage rate measures, and SDAs were never worse off for increasing average employment or wages among participants. The individual centers tracked the labor market outcomes of their participants based on federal and state guidelines. At the end of each program year, states calculated the performance measures for each center, along with the bonus to which it was entitled. A center could receive nothing or, if it exceeded the standards, could receive a bonus amounting to as much as 20 to 30 percent of its regular budget. The bonus funds were valuable to centers because they were fungible and could be used with more flexibility than regular program funds could.

How JTPA Worked in Practice

A number of studies have examined the performance of JTPA, the challenges it faced in coming up with reasonable measures of performance, and the implications of these measures in terms of provider behavior. Their findings offer valuable lessons for the design and implementation of an accountability system using performance standards and incentives. We first discuss the measures of performance used by JTPA and then discuss how these measures affected provider behavior.

Measures of Performance

Generally, performance standards based on short-term outcome levels are less expensive than measures based on long-term effects because they rely on straightforward calculations using administrative data. Two factors influenced the choice of performance measures: the need to keep measurement costs low and the need to give training managers at the SDAs rapid feedback on their performance. These factors led designers of the JTPA incentive system at the federal level to choose a set of short-term labor-market measures based on an enrollee's employment status, wage, and earnings (Courty and Marschke, 1997, p. 384). The choice of performance measures had a less-than-optimum influence on provider behavior. One major problem in using short-run outcome measures is that it may focus attention on criteria that do not promote long-run benefits. For example, training may encourage the further pursuit of education and/or training that may delay entrance into the labor market and hence depress measured employment and earnings in the short run but raise them in the long run. In many cases, the short-term outcome measures were weakly and negatively related to longer-term participant earnings and employment gains that were the focus of the JTPA (Heckman, Heinrich, and Smith, forthcoming).

Effects on Provider Behavior

Cream Skimming. According to Section 141 (c), JTPA was to be targeted to *those who can benefit from, and who are most in need of* employment and training opportunities (http://www.doleta.gov/regs/statutes/jtpalaw.asp). Unfortunately, the evidence strongly suggests that defining performance standards in terms of short-term outcome measures did not encourage training centers to provide services to those who were most in need and could have benefited from them. Providers often have private information related to outcomes that is not available to the state managers, so, for example, they may know more about the employability of their applicants than the state does. Under JTPA, training centers received the same credit regardless of whether they enrolled and placed an individual with limited skills or someone who was an accomplished student (Cragg, 1995). DOL attempted to correct for this by introducing a set of adjustments that statistically corrected for observable differences in the applicants. However, these adjustments did not correct for applicant ability and prior work experiences, characteristics that were readily available to the training providers.

Heckman, Heinrich, and Smith (forthcoming) define *cream skimming* in the context of performance standards as selecting (or enrolling) people who help attain short-term goals rather than selecting those who would gain the most in the long run. Evidence of cream skimming by training centers comes from several studies. For example, Anderson et al. (1992) showed that less-educated eligible individuals tended to be underrepresented in the program and estimated that if eligible persons participated at random, the placement rate would be significantly lower. Heckman and Smith (1995) found similar evidence suggesting that adults with less than ten years of schooling had lower probabilities of reaching the application, acceptance, and enrollment stage. However, in a study of an individual center in Texas, there was evidence of *negative* cream skimming by staff, who apparently selected the most disadvantaged applicants to enroll because of their own preferences for helping the needy (Heckman, Smith, and Taber, 1996).

Another study used the variation in state characteristics to investigate whether these characteristics contributed to cream skimming. It found that: (a) in states with higher unemployment rates, cream-skimming led to more experienced applicants being much more likely to be enrolled; (b) in states with more-intensive incentives, more-able individuals were likely to be selected; (c) in states with policies that adjusted for participant characteristics, less-experienced individuals were selected into the JTPA program. In states with high incentives *and* an adjustment policy, individuals with lower experience were much more likely to be enrolled (Cragg, 1995).

Manipulation of the Reporting Data. In addition to cream skimming, the fact that training centers had discretion over the termination and reporting dates may have led them to "game the system." At the end of the training period, the training centers faced two options: report the enrollee's labor market outcomes or postpone the reporting date in the hope that the outcomes would improve. Training centers under JTPA received all or most of their award for simply meeting state-defined standards. This provided an incentive to postpone reporting outcomes for unemployed enrollees and then, in the last month, to draw down this inventory when the achievement of the standard was assured. There is evidence that training centers attempted to maximize their performance by manipulating the reporting date and piling up reporting of unemployed enrollees toward the end of the program year (Courty and Marschke, forthcoming). Training centers offered special services, such as transportation, child care, clothing allowance during the 90-day follow-up period, and case managers sought to influence employers to keep clients employed at least until the 90-day period had elapsed. Training centers did exactly what they were told and no more; they made no attempts to contact clients or offer further placement or counseling services after the follow-up period had expired.

Overview of the Workforce Investment Act[2,3]

The Workforce Investment Act (WIA), passed by Congress in 1998, attempted to address some of the shortcomings of the JTPA by establishing new outcome measures. However, states faced several challenges in implementing WIA, some of which are similar to those facing states struggling with accountability provisions under NCLB.

Concerned that the employment and training system was so fragmented, WIA brought together 17 programs—including the three JTPA Title I programs—provided by four federal agencies. All services were now to be provided through a one-stop-center system. The three new WIA programs that replaced the JTPA programs offer a broader range of services and no longer use income to determine eligibility for all program services. Services range from basic services, such as providing information on job markets or helping with job searches, to more intensive services, such as comprehensive assessment and case management. Only those job seekers who receive these intensive services are included in the performance measures.

WIA is designed to provide greater accountability than JTPA by establishing new outcome measures and requiring states to use Unemployment Insurance (UI) data to track and report on the performance of the three JTPA-replacement programs. The performance measures now explicitly include skill attainment and customer satisfaction to provide a better measure of the kinds of skills that indi-

---

[2] See http://www.doleta.gov/usworkforce/asp/wialaw.pdf.

[3] Because our focus in this report is on JTPA, we provide only a very brief overview of the WIA and selected early findings on its implementation that seemed to have some relevance for education. Time and budget constraints did not permit a more detailed examination of how WIA is working in practice.

viduals attain and to ascertain whether participants are satisfied with the services. JTPA established expected performance levels by using a computer model. Under WIA, however, these expected performance levels are negotiated between states and DOL; in turn, states negotiate performance levels with each local area. The starting point for these negotiations is estimates from historical data that take into account differences in economic conditions, participants, and services provided.

States are expected to meet the set goals every year. A state that fails to meet its performance level for one year is provided with technical assistance; after two consecutive years of failure, it may be subject to a 5-percent reduction in its annual WIA grant. If states meet or exceed expected performance levels, they are eligible to receive incentive grants that generally range from $750,000 to $3 million.

Early Implementation of the WIA

The U.S. General Accounting Office (GAO) reviewed the implementation and effectiveness of WIA in 2001 (United States General Accounting Office, 2002). It found that states faced a number of challenges in implementing the new system. Because of the new data requirements, most states decided to develop new automated systems; as of 2001, however, 15 states did not have systems completely in place. The GAO also found that the new performance measures were complex and required a considerable amount of resources. For example, states had to implement complicated procedures to measure customer satisfaction through surveys. Additionally, states reported that they were not sure who to include in the measures, when to collect the data for the measures, and how to calculate the measures. Another concern was that some state officials viewed the levels of performance as too high and out of touch with local economic conditions. Because there are financial sanctions attached to failure, states may engage in cream skimming by choosing to serve only those job seekers with the best prospects of finding work.

WIA performance measures may not provide a true picture of WIA-funded programs largely because of the lack of timeliness or comparability of data across states. For example, DOL's guidance on who should be tracked and included was not clear, so states and localities differed on whom they tracked and when. In addition, the lack of a definition of "credential" also caused differences in the way this indicator was measured across states.

Implications for Education

Unlike the two models discussed earlier (the Baldrige Award Program and TPS), the JTPA, WIA, and NCLB focus on outcomes, not the process by which those outcomes are produced. Thus, the lessons from the outcome-focused JTPA and WIA regarding the challenges inherent in designing efficient and workable performance incentives are applicable to test-based accountability systems like NCLB.

Explicit Performance Objectives May Produce Mixed Outcomes

The JTPA example highlights the relationship between outcome measures and provider behavior. In systems with performance standards, organizations usually get what they pay for. Outcomes tied to financial incentives are likely to improve, increasing productivity; but other activities may be performed in less-efficient ways that are not beneficial (Holmstrom and Milgrom, 1991).

Evidence from the JTPA experience suggested that providers did not behave in quite the way that Congress had expected. Providers chose to enroll applicants who had greater employment prospects or those who could earn higher wages rather than targeting services to those most in need. This was a direct outcome of the weight given to these two outcome measures in determining rewards. Similarly, NCLB concentrates on student test scores as the single measure of performance, and there are rewards and sanctions associated with either meeting or failing to meet the target goals. If states, schools, and teachers are judged on the basis of test scores, they will concentrate on activities or strategies that will lead to higher test scores. These strategies and behaviors are likely to be both desirable and undesirable.

On the one hand, a focus on high-stakes testing may motivate students to work harder, support better diagnosis of individual student needs, help teachers identify areas of strength and weakness in the curriculum, lead teachers to align instruction with standards, help administrators judge the quality of their program and lead them to change school policies to improve curriculum and instruction (Stecher, 2001).

On the other hand, such a focus may lead to a variety of dysfunctional behaviors. For example, if (as with the WIA) state officials are concerned that current levels of performance are set too high, they may be tempted to resort to setting cut scores low, choosing a minimum competency test, or encouraging more parent waivers, exclusions from testing, or even dropouts. This would seriously undermine the intent of the law, which is to ensure that students are being held (and taught) to high standards. Another counterproductive behavior may occur when there are sanctions attached to failure (as in the JTPA). Schools may engage in a form of cream skimming by focusing only on those students who have the best prospects of passing the state tests, often referred to as "bubble kids"—students whose scores are close to the proficiency cut-scores and who might move up with a little extra work. Schools may also encourage students to stay at home on the day of testing or place difficult students in categories that exempt them from testing. Teachers may spend more time on specific test content or inappropriate test preparation, reducing the time spent on other topics and effectively narrowing the curriculum. In a worst-case scenario, teachers may resort to cheating in response to the focus on test scores. It is also possible that administrators will enact policies that increase test scores but not necessarily increase learning.

Given the experience of other performance standards systems and the evidence of cream skimming and other forms of dysfunctional behavior in the JTPA and now under the WIA, performance systems need to be carefully monitored and changed if the incentives and outcome measures lead to undesirable behavior. Similarly, the federal government needs to monitor NCLB carefully as it is implemented in the various states, particularly in light of the latitude given to states to determine their own standards and tests.

Data Collection Alone Does Not Drive Improvement

As we saw earlier, the GAO (2002) reported that WIA placed heavy demands on states in terms of data requirements and capacity for analysis. The new performance measures were complex and required manipulation of the UI database. In addition, states had to implement surveys to measure consumer satisfaction. These findings echo some of the problems states are facing in implementing the new accountability systems under NCLB. Like the WIA, NCLB requires states and districts to put into place systems to track and analyze assessment data. The new guidance for defining adequate yearly progress (AYP) for schools and the need to disaggregate student outcome data by groups of students are complex and require a fair amount of resources.

Whether the capacity exists at the state, district, and school level to analyze the data and use them for continuous improvement is an open question that needs careful monitoring. We have no clear evidence that the service delivery centers, under either JTPA or WIA, used the data they provided the states to actually improve services and outcomes. Schools are more complex than training centers, and it takes much more effort, time, and resources to improve student performance—and ultimately school performance—than to improve the employment prospects of adults. In an era of constrained state budgets with scarce resources, funding for education may be reduced. If data are not available to support school decisionmaking and schools do not know how to use these data, regardless of their availability, it is unlikely that such information could be the key driver of change that NCLB assumes it to be.

Educational Systems Should Use Multiple Measures of Performance

Focusing on short-term outcome measures risks diverting attention from long-term issues. As mentioned earlier, training may encourage further training and schooling, which may depress employment and earnings measures in the short run but raise them in the long run. Focusing exclusively on short-term measures may thus be counterproductive.

Similarly, if the focus in NCLB is on improving mathematics and reading, it is likely that other subjects—such as social studies, science, or music and art—may be given less time and emphasis. Given constrained budgets, funding for what are seen as "electives" may be reduced or eliminated. If that is so, then one desired outcome of schooling—that children receive a broad-based education that prepares them for citizenship and participation in the democratic process—is not likely to occur. Even in mathematics and reading, emphasis may shift toward the topics and the formats that are included on tests. For example, if reading is tested using short passages and multiple-choice questions, reading instruction may downplay longer passages and other types of questions.

Nor is it clear whether these short-term outcome measures reflect the longer-term outcomes that presumably are the ultimate goal of schooling—ensuring that each student has a chance to lead a successful and productive life. For example, Heckman, Heinrich, and Smith (forthcoming) found that, under JTPA, the short-term outcome measures were weakly and negatively related to participants' longer-term earnings and employment gains. There appears to be a positive relationship between performance on reading and mathematics tests in K–12 and postsecondary and labor market outcomes (Murnane, Willett, and Levy, 1995), but the mechanism through which the former influences the latter is not well understood. We must examine the relationship between short-term and longer-term outcomes and identify the strategies that appear to be most successful in translating one into the other. If we focus on outcomes and ignore process, we may know that the school is failing but not know why it is failing.

The JTPA Framework Highlights the Need to Adjust for Differences in Ability

JTPA and WIA both offer some adjustments and incentives for harder-to-place enrollees. Educators are of two minds when it comes to recognizing the need for some form of ability/effort adjustment in AYP measures. Students have varying abilities, pose different challenges, and require different levels of effort (and resources) on the part of schools and teachers to bring them up to required levels of proficiency—and outcome measures must reflect these differences. However, since the 1994 reauthorization of the ESEA, it has been an article of faith that all students can master challenging content and complex problem-solving skills and that all students need to be held to the same high standards. There is thus an implicit assumption that the level of effort necessary to bring a student to proficiency is the same, regardless of the student's ability. Under the earliest version of the JTPA, training centers received the same credit for enrolling and placing hard-to-place individuals as for individuals with greater skills. Later, DOL attempted to correct for this by adjusting for observable differences in the applicants, although the variables did not completely measure prior work experience and applicant ability. As a result, training centers engaged in some form of cream skimming, especially in states with higher unemployment rates and higher incentives.

There are no easy answers to this dilemma or indeed to the question of how best to account for differences in ability, but if teachers are to be held accountable for the learning outcomes of every student, it is an issue that needs careful study. We return to this issue in Chapter Seven, where we discuss the use of specific models of risk-adjustment to account for differences in the health status of patients.

CHAPTER FIVE

Accountability in the Legal Profession

Heather Barney

Many authors have advocated professional accountability in education as offering the most promise for the advancement of teaching and improvement of student learning (Darling-Hammond and Ascher, 1991; O'Reilly, 1996; Adams and Kirst, 1998; O'Day, 2002). *Professional accountability* is any system by which members of a given profession provide regulation and oversight to the practice of their trade. In this chapter, we examine how professional accountability is structured in mature professions, using the legal profession as an example, and discuss the implications for education. We begin by reviewing briefly the nature of professions in general before turning to a description of accountability in the legal profession. The final section draws out the lessons learned for educational accountability.

The Nature of Professions

The nature of professions has been a topic of significant interest to scholars over the years. Throughout the first half of the 20th century, numerous sociologists put forward definitions of a profession, generally based on a list of attributes or traits that were common to existing professions such as law and medicine (see, for example, Flexner, 1915; Greenwood, 1957; Barber, 1963; Millerson, 1964; Carr-Saunders and Wilson, 1933; Lieberman, 1956; Goode, 1957). Although these definitions differed somewhat, nearly all included a number of common points: Professions involve the application of specialized knowledge in nonroutine ways; the work of professionals has an element of altruism or community interest to it; and professionals are organized into autonomous, self-governing bodies.

By the late 1970s, however, this method of defining professions based on attributes had been called into question. Some critics pointed out that the criteria were difficult to apply in concrete situations, making distinctions between occupations seem arbitrary and subject to political or cultural bias. As Dingwall (1976, p. 332) concluded, "the logical outcome of this approach is that a profession is nothing more or less than what some sociologist says it is." More problematic, the process of defining a profession by ensuring that those occupations that were commonly thought to be professions fit the definition while those not so regarded did not was viewed as merely reinforcing the status quo. Roth (1974, p. 6) argued that such an approach "decoyed students of occupations into becoming apologists for the professionalism ideology, justifying the professionals' control over their work situation." Later scholars thus came to focus more on the process by which some occupations became professions and on what purpose professions served.

Burk (2002), one contemporary scholar, offers his own working definition:

> A profession is a relatively "high status" occupation whose members apply abstract knowledge to solve problems in a particular field of endeavor. (p. 21)

His definition emphasizes three factors that together mark an occupation as a profession: expertise or mastery of abstract knowledge, which generally comes about through higher education; control over a jurisdiction within which members of the profession attempt to apply their expert knowledge; and legitimacy—the source of professional status—that comes about when such expertise is validated by the client and forms the basis of trust between the profession and the society it serves. Once such trust is established, professions are granted some limited autonomy to establish and enforce their own professional ethics, the maintenance of which further enhances such trust. (Snider and Watkins, 2002, p. 7)

Abbott (1988) argues that an occupation's identification as a profession and its status are outcomes of competition within a system of professions for control over abstract knowledge applied within specific jurisdictions. Professions wage this war by various means, from redefining the nature of the professional task to lobbying for legislation that bars others from doing work in the field (for example, preventing those who have not passed the bar examination from practicing as lawyers). Burk (2002) points out that the most important factor for gaining and maintaining control over a jurisdiction is a clear demonstration that the professional activity succeeds—that is, it solves the problems with which it was faced. Burk's work is fairly typical of the more cynical view scholars in more recent years have taken of professions.

The traditional definitions of professions and the more contemporary ones are not so different as to be mutually exclusive. They differ in perspective more than in substance, with earlier researchers viewing professions more benevolently, whereas recent scholars take a more cynical approach and regard professions as significantly less benign than their predecessors did. Both groups agree on the importance of complex knowledge and specialized skills. Recent scholars such as Burk (2002) would disagree with earlier researchers' emphasis on altruism and community interest among professionals. They acknowledge, however, that professionals often perform what at least seem like community-oriented acts, although they would argue that they do so because of a self-interested need to maintain the public trust that underlies their profession's legitimacy (see Collins and Jacobs, 2002). Similarly, both groups agree on a need for self-regulation by their professions, but whereas earlier sociologists saw this need as a benevolent act intended to protect the public, more-recent scholars regard it as part of a self-interested system designed to inflate salaries by excluding outsiders.

These definitions of profession are important for education be-cause they have implications for the ability to establish and rely on professional accountability to improve teaching and learning. We have generally taken a less cynical view of professionalism than many recent theorists because our goal in this document is to seek out promising ideas and best practices from other fields. Yet we are also mindful of the discrepancy between professional accountability as a benevolent theoretical ideal and professional accountability as it has in fact developed in many professions. In the discussion that follows, we highlight areas that would be of particular concern to educational policymakers seeking to implement a system of professional account-ability.

Overview of Accountability in the Legal Profession

From the many theoretical considerations of professions, we can de-rive several propositions that might underlie a system of professional accountability. Three of them seem most important for our consid-eration of the legal and teaching professions: deference from clients and the public to practitioners' professional authority; a pervasive sense of professional responsibility among all practitioners; and an interest and duty among all practitioners for the self-policing of the profession and of fellow practitioners. In the legal profession, these propositions manifest themselves through a comprehensive set of regulations that control entry into the profession, mandate capacity-building, investigate and prosecute disciplinary infractions, and offer nondisciplinary means of addressing and redressing client concerns. The specific details of accountability systems vary across states, but all jurisdictions include some manifestation of each of these four com-ponents in their systems.

Professional Authority

Adams and Kirst (1998, p. 469) note that "deference to expertise constitutes the operating dynamic" of professional accountability. The assumption is that laypersons ought to give deference to the professional authority of the trained practitioner. This deference arises from and depends on a widely held belief that the profession is complex and requires both specialized skills and abstract knowledge that only professional training can impart and the discretion to apply those skills in a nonroutine manner that accommodates the individual needs and context of each client (Millerson, 1964; Barber, 1963; Flexner, 1915; Carr-Saunders and Wilson, 1933; Burk, 2002). The existence of a specialized, distinct knowledge base and the mastery of that knowledge base by all those authorized to practice in the profession—or at least a public perception to that effect—are thus key to any system of professional accountability.

Careful controls on entry into the legal profession, as well as requirements for continuous professional development (discussed further below), ensure that those who are given the right to practice law have demonstrated an initial mastery of the specialized legal knowledge base and an ongoing effort to maintain and expand that mastery throughout their careers. For lawyers, clearing the hurdle set by these requirements seems effective to ensure a strong degree of public deference. While some incompetent lawyers do manage to enter practice, few would argue that the majority of lawyers are poorly educated or that they are not significantly better equipped to navigate the complex legal system than others without specific training in the law. The greater concern may be that, as Carl Sandburg wrote, "The Lawyers Know Too Much." Contemporary professions' scholars do, however, note the negative potential for entry requirements to serve as a bar that keeps the numbers within the profession artificially low to preserve business for existing professionals and to inflate their salaries rather than as a legitimate gatekeeping mechanism to exclude only unqualified candidates.

Controls on Entry

Entry into the legal profession is controlled through a set of requirements for licensure. In most cases, the state board of examiners, a panel of legal experts, sets rules for licensure, although the state high court or the state legislature grants formal authorizing power for the board's policies. Unauthorized-practice laws, which prohibit individuals who are not licensed from practicing law on behalf of others, legitimize the entry requirements and grant them power. In addition to licensure requirements, 34 states also restrict law practice to members of their "unified" bar associations, the professional organizations of attorneys in the state (http://www.abanet.org). Requirements for licensure and admission to the bar generally consist of three components: educational requirements, a licensure exam, and a test of moral character and fitness.

In nearly all cases, lawyers are required to have obtained the Juris Doctor degree from an approved school of law.[1] Although a few states have their own accreditation systems, in the majority of states schools gain approval through accreditation by the American Bar Association (ABA), a national voluntary professional organization for legal practitioners (NCBE and ABA, 2002). ABA accreditation is based on criteria related to the school's organization and administration, program of legal education, faculty, admissions processes and services, library and information resources, and facilities (ABA Section, 2002). As of September 2002, there were 187 ABA-approved programs, enrolling 132,901 students (http://www.abanet.org).

Following completion of the degree, prospective lawyers must pass a licensure exam consisting of both multiple choice and essay questions covering topical content matter and, in some states, performance issues and professional responsibility. Nearly all states test candidates using a series of standardized multistate exams developed by American College Testing in consultation with the National Conference of Board Examiners, a nonprofit corporation composed of state bar examiners and unaffiliated with the ABA. Passing scores vary by state and are often based on formulas that make comparison of standards across states difficult (NCBE and ABA, 2002). In 2001, 66 percent of all candidates taking the licensure exam passed, with state pass rates ranging from 50 percent in California to 92 percent in South Dakota (NCBE, 2002).

---

[1] In 2001, 90 percent of bar examinees were graduates of state approved law schools. Just 48 out of more than 70,000 had not completed formal law study (NCBE, 2002).

In addition to passing the licensure exam, prospective lawyers must also demonstrate satisfactory moral character and fitness. Almost half the states have published character and fitness standards, requiring applicants to have such qualities as honesty, trustworthiness, diligence, and reliability. Conduct that might be considered to reflect a deficiency in character and fitness includes unlawful conduct, academic dishonesty, neglect of financial responsibilities, evidence of mental or emotional instability, and dependence on drugs or alcohol. Neither the process for determining fitness nor the standards are particularly rigorous; for example, only five states regard a felony conviction as an automatic bar to licensure (NCBE and ABA, 2002).

Alternative Legal Training

In recent years, a movement has developed to challenge the strict controls on entry in the legal profession. Advocates such as HALT, a non-partisan public interest group for legal reform, and Nolo, a legal publishing company, have argued that current controls on entry and unauthorized-practice laws have granted monopoly power to the "lawyer cartel" and made basic legal services unaffordable for many Americans. The advocacy groups have sought alternative options. As a result of their work, California recently enacted the nation's first Legal Document Assistant program, whereby practitioners with limited training may assist clients with certain routine legal tasks and may file documents on their behalf. In addition, bookstores nationwide now carry Nolo's self-help law books, which offer standardized examples of documents—wills, power-of-attorney, and so on—that customers can adapt for their own use with minimal aid from an attorney.

Yet these developments have not been widely regarded as a major attack on the professional authority of lawyers or the efficacy of their professional accountability system. Lawyers have been at least somewhat tolerant because the critics distinguish between tasks that are complex enough to be the exclusive province of professionals and those that are routine and standardized enough to require just minimal training.

Continuous Professional Development

Beyond the entry requirements, the accountability system also demands that all lawyers continue to expand their knowledge and skills throughout the course of their careers, so that practitioners remain current with the latest additions to their profession's specialized knowledge base. Most states impose mandatory continuing legal education requirements on bar members ranging from eight to fifteen hours per year and generally covering such topics as ethics, substance abuse prevention, professionalism, and office practice skills (NCBE, 2002). A handful of states have also recently instituted "bridge-the-gap" courses or apprenticeship programs to help beginning lawyers through their induction into the profession. In addition, many state bar associations offer hotlines and workshops for members to help them deal with such issues as law office management, ethics, mental health, and substance abuse and dependency. A few states' bar associations are also developing mentoring programs for both new and experienced lawyers (Conference of Chief Justices, 1999).

Professional Responsibility

A second important assumption underlying systems of professional accountability is the notion that the practitioners operating within those systems have a professional responsibility to protect the public. Altruistic service was long held to be a defining characteristic of professions by sociologists in the first half of the 20th century. As Becker (1962) points out, "The symbol of the profession . . . portrays a group whose members have altruistic motivations and whose professional activities are governed by a code of ethics which heavily emphasizes devotion to service and the good of the client" (see also Millerson, 1964). Even a cynic such as Burk (2002, p. 35) acknowledges that while the notion of professionals as "social trustees" has been seriously eroded in the past half century, "one cannot explain or justify self-sacrifice for the public good that . . . professional service often requires" through the language of market-oriented self-interest; rather, it must be justified in the language of morality. From a less lofty perspective, professional responsibility can be seen as the required quid pro quo for the monopoly power states grant to professionals through statutes regulating entry, particularly if members of the profession themselves have a hand in shaping such regulations. Zemans and Rosenblum (1981, p. 165) argue that "states grant monopoly power to professional groups ostensibly both to facilitate better service for their clientele and to better serve the public good. At a minimum this would seem to require consideration of how one's actions affect the public good." Whether as a moral obligation inherent to all professions or as a balance for monopoly power, systems of professional accountability demand a strong sense of professional responsibility.

Addressing and Protecting Client Concerns

In the legal profession, the most obvious mechanism for demonstrating professional responsibility is through the client protection trusts that state bar associations fund out of member dues and maintain to reimburse clients who lose money as the result of an attorney's dishonest conduct (Conference of Chief Justices, 1999). In practical terms, lawyer compensation funds have been a relatively weak component of accountability systems in many states. Three states limit fund recovery payments to just $5,000 per victim. Not a single claim was made against New Hampshire's fund in the first four years of its existence because the fund had never been publicized (http://www.nolo.com).

Another problem is that funds generally cover only dishonest conduct, not incompetence. Still, the funds do have the potential for playing an important symbolic role. Distributing restitution payments on behalf of the collective profession to compensate for the incompetent or unethical behavior of individual members provides a symbolic measure of responsibility among members of the profession for the welfare of the public. The profession acknowledges the potential for lawyers to cause harm and creates a financial incentive for individual lawyers to take a broader view of the profession and its place in society than their own practice provides. Forcing members of the bar to collectively bear financial responsibility for the actions of all those in the profession also symbolically demonstrates the membership's confidence in the accountability system and encourages lawyers to take on greater responsibility for "policing their own" to ensure that they are not forced to pay compensation for system failures.

Another means of instilling a sense of professional responsibility in practitioners are guidelines for *pro bono* service to be rendered by all licensed attorneys—although, with a few exceptions, such guidelines are entirely voluntary and carry no disciplinary implications. Though other mechanisms for impelling lawyers to take on professional responsibility involve financial consideration, additional resources such as arbitration and mediation services offered by the state bar also help protect the public by offering lawyers' clients ways to deal with minor disagreements and complaints such as billing disputes (ABA Center, 1992).

Collective Self-Regulation

The third major assumption underlying systems of professional accountability is that the professions should have the collective capability and will to regulate and police themselves. A self-enforced code of conduct was one of the most commonly cited attributes of professions in the work of mid–20th century sociologists (see Carr-Saunders and Wilson, 1933; Greenwood, 1957; Millerson, 1964). The need for self-policing of practitioners under professional accountability is the logical corollary of professional responsibility and professional authority. Protecting the public entails removing from the profession those who would do harm, while monopoly power over specialized and complex knowledge implies that professionals themselves ought to be uniquely suited to judge the competence and skill with which others apply that knowledge.

Since self-policing also serves the self-interest of practitioners themselves by allowing them to enhance the credibility of their profession by removing those whose actions serve to bring their collective image into disrepute, more-recent theorists, too, acknowledge the need for professions to exercise self-regulation. As Collins and Jacobs (2002, p. 40) point out, "For the body as a whole to remain respected and privileged as a profession, the body must police itself to ensure that client exploitation does not occur. In this way, the individual members are constrained to conform to standards of ethical conduct that protect the body as a whole."

Lawyer Discipline System

In the legal profession, self-policing is guided by clearly articulated procedures for disciplinary enforcement developed by the profession itself through professional organizations like the ABA. Although the system does not quite involve true self-policing, the legal profession does play a significant role in the process.

The ABA Model Rules, which guide accountability policies in most states, offer an overview of how self-policing is typically accomplished in practical terms. The lawyer disciplinary system should be overseen by an independent state agency, with laypersons accounting for a third of the membership and practicing members of the bar filling the rest of the seats. The agency and its members should be authorized and appointed by the state high court. A centralized administrative unit of the agency should deal with intake of client complaints and initial determinations as to whether the allegations, if true, amount to a breach of standards that would warrant disciplinary action. The role of investigating allegations and prosecuting cases should be carried out by the office of the states' Disciplinary Counsel, a bar member who is appointed by the state high court and devotes his or her full-time attention to the disciplinary system. Under the Model Rules, cases should be heard by rotating three-person panels consisting of two state bar members and one layperson, all appointed by the state agency. The hearing panels should present recommendations on cases to the agency, which in turn should present recommendations to the state high court, with which ultimate authority lies. Sanctions for misconduct include private admonitions, public reprimands, restitution, suspension, limitations on future practice, and disbarment and revocation of a lawyer's license (ABA Standing Committee, 2002).

Notably, this system does not provide for ongoing monitoring but rather assumes that a licensed lawyer is practicing competently and ethically unless a complaint is filed that indicates otherwise.

Market Forces

Finally, it is worthwhile noting that 80 percent of practicing licensed attorneys in the United States are employed in private law practice, and an additional 10 percent work in private industry. For the vast majority of lawyers, the formal accountability system grants a stamp of approval that they have met certain standards, but their skill and competency beyond these minimum criteria are ultimately judged by the marketplace. Firms have a relatively free hand to exercise discretion over personnel decisions, and consumers have a full range of choices as to the firms with which they wish to do business. Information plays an important role in any market.

Although the ability of consumers to discern between good and bad lawyers is hindered somewhat by a lack of meaningful and quantifiable outcome measures, a system of lawyer ratings helps to at least partially fill this gap, although the effectiveness of the ratings and their use remains a matter open for debate. The Martindale-Hubbell ratings, in use since 1896, draw upon confidential opinions of bar members and include assessments of each lawyer's legal ability and adherence to professional standards of conduct and ethics. The ratings are designed as positive indicators of a lawyer's reputation and skill, although the fact that there are no negative ratings makes it difficult for consumers to distinguish between lawyers who have been denied ratings and those who have simply not yet gone through the review process. As of 2002, 45 percent of U.S. lawyers in private practice had been reviewed and assigned a positive rating (http://www.martindale.com).

Applying the Legal Model to Educational Accountability

The comparison of legal practice to teaching is in many ways appropriate because there are a number of parallels between the two. Both provide services whose outcomes are often difficult to quantify. In education, researchers continue to argue over the definition and measurement of student achievement; in law, outcomes may be even more nebulous and may vary from client to client, from maximizing monetary net future gains to ensuring child custody to minimizing liabilities or prison time.

Even where outcomes can be agreed upon and quantified, in both fields they are likely to be influenced by factors beyond the practitioners' control. Test scores, for example, may be due in part to family or community factors, while a trial lawyer's win/loss record depends not only on his skill, but also on the actual guilt or innocence of his clients, the quality of related police investigations, the final makeup of the jury, and so on. Finally, both education and legal practice are essentially public pursuits with special ties to the state. The majority of teachers work in government-funded schools with clients who are bound by law to partake of their services until a specified age; lawyers are granted unique privileges to practice in the courts of the judicial branch and engage primarily in interpreting and applying government laws and regulations.

The analogy is not perfect, or course, and a few caveats should be kept in mind when comparing teaching and legal practice. Measuring losses or gains related to exceptionally good or bad teaching practice and translating them into financial terms is significantly more challenging in education than in law. In part, this is because education is a nonmonetary good that is inherently difficult to value. In addition, the number of teachers a student has over the course of twelve years of schooling makes the attribution of losses or gains to particular teachers nearly impossible. In contrast, lawyers can profit from their work more easily than teachers can, which affects the balance between self-interest and public interest in these two fields. A final important difference is the fact that, in contrast with teachers, lawyers have been trained in the skills needed to navigate laws and regulations and the court system and are thus uniquely suited to play both prosecutorial and defense roles in an adversarial accountability system. Professional organizations for lawyers can properly side with prosecutors in disciplinary cases because accused attorneys are presumably well equipped by their training to protect their own legal rights over the course of the proceedings.

Educators, policymakers, and other stakeholders should also bear in mind that, while the current system of lawyer discipline is effective in many ways, it continually confronts a major problem in terms of public credibility. Although systems of self-regulation provide benefits by empowering those with the most knowledge of the profession to judge the performance of others in the profession, they also provide for significant appearances of conflicts of interest and thus may provoke considerable public mistrust. This can be dealt with to some extent by a careful partitioning of adjudicative and prosecutorial functions among different entities. However, the functioning of lawyer discipline systems in most states to date has done little to dispel such notions. One study found that only 5 percent of the complaints nationwide result in discipline, meaning that the vast majority of concerns that the public takes seriously enough to take formal action on are dismissed by the system (Kraus, 2000). Such statistics no doubt cast considerable doubt on the effectiveness of professional accountability as currently implemented in the legal profession and highlight the need for policymakers to carefully consider and refine the ways in which theoretically sound ideas may be exercised in practice should such a system be replicated in education.

The underlying question of whether teaching technically qualifies as a profession in the same model as legal practice has been much debated. Teaching is generally not among the "classical" professions that were much studied in the mid–20th century, though a few scholars do include educators as professionals. As theorists have in recent years moved away from the definitions and models of professionalism that had been developed in the mid–20th century, some scholars have argued that the entire question of whether teaching is a profession is now irrelevant (see, for example, Runte, 1995). Whatever the answer to this theoretical question, among educators the move toward professionalization and calls for professional accountability have been real and prominent, so lessons learned from the example of the legal profession offer important insights for ongoing discussions about accountability in education.

Implications for Education

The Knowledge Base in Education is Not Yet Sufficiently Well-Regarded for Professional Accountability

In education, a number of efforts have been made to implement a system of certification that would include many components similar to those used by the legal profession.[2] For example, teacher candidates in most states must receive their degree from a state-approved college or university, much as most lawyers are required to earn a degree from an ABA-accredited law school. Thirty-six states have adopted the standards of the National Council for Accreditation of Teacher Education as their state unit standards, and all but nine states have instituted mandatory testing on basic skills, pedagogy, and content knowledge for teacher certification, similar to the bar exams for lawyers. Most states require fingerprinting and background checks, and many request written recommendations from candidates' teacher education programs, similar to character and fitness testing for lawyers (U.S. Department of Education, 2002). Continuous professional development is now a standard component of teachers' responsibilities. Nearly all teacher workshops and seminars address issues directly related to classroom instruction as opposed to the courses on ethics and substance abuse that lawyers are required to take. As a result, educators may actually have better avenues for capacity-building than lawyers do.

Still, the requirements for entry into the teaching profession have become the subject of considerable debate and controversy. Teachers are allowed to work in private schools and many charter schools without meeting any of the requirements for certification in their state, while alternative certification programs seek to place teachers in the classroom with only minimal preservice training in

---

[2] There is a difference between licensure (which is the standard in the legal profession) and certification (which applies in education). Licensure sets a minimum standard for anyone practicing in a profession, and practice by an unlicensed person is illegal. Certification confers special status, but it is not a universal requirement for practice. For example, individuals can teach in a private school without receiving a state certification.

education. Critics of teacher education regard certification requirements not as useful indicators of mastery of a specialized knowledge base as in the legal profession but as "hoops and hurdles" unrelated to improved teacher quality (U.S. Department of Education, 2002). Viewed in light of the similar requirements used in the legal profession, these criticisms of teacher certification suggest that controls on entry into a profession are a necessary but not sufficient factor in ensuring deference to professional authority. Lawyers certainly could not expect to be regarded as experts in their field if their profession were unable to screen out those who had not demonstrated a mastery of legal skills and knowledge. However, such screening would be meaningless without acknowledgement of the fact that those skills and knowledge are complex and specialized and thus inaccessible to the untrained public.

Successful teaching may indeed require a distinct and specialized knowledge base that is similarly inaccessible to those without specific training in education and pedagogy. If this is the case, however, that knowledge base has to date been understated at the very least and is more likely underdeveloped. The answer to whether teacher certification requirements are important markers of specialized mastery or "hoops and hurdles" will ultimately lie with researchers and their findings regarding the nature of successful teaching and related skills and characteristics. For now, many people have perceptions of teaching—the "those who can't, teach" belief—that are incompatible with an effective system of professional accountability. In terms of the definition of professionalism laid out by Burk (2002) at the beginning of this chapter, teachers suffer from a serious lack of legitimacy because the general public does not perceive their specialized knowledge to be effective. These perceptions would have to be dispelled through strong research on and articulation of the skills and knowledge required for demonstrably successful teaching before a certification system could flourish and gain state support as it has in the legal profession.

Professional Accountability and Alternative Certification Can Coexist

The relationship between licensed attorneys and groups like HALT and Nolo, as well as the new Legal Document Assistant program in California, suggests the possibility of a middle ground between those who call for even tighter controls on entry into teaching and those who call for radically streamlined certification systems. In the legal profession, the notable factor enabling the coexistence of professional accountability and alternative training was the agreed-upon distinction between tasks that did, in fact, require professional discretion and specialized knowledge and those that were routine.

In education, this might suggest that nontraditional pathways into the classroom and professional accountability could coexist if a similar division of labor were enacted. Fully educated and certified teachers would exercise professional discretion in complex, context-dependent tasks, whereas those with lesser professional training performed more routine tasks, as teacher aides often do now. Those with specialized knowledge in complementary areas, such as career-changers with advanced degrees in math or science, might work collaboratively with professionally trained teachers to create effective content area curriculum and instruction through the combination of their respective expertise.

Educators Should Foster a Sense of Public Responsibility

Instilling professional responsibility is an important practice that educators, like lawyers, might do well to imitate in their own systems of professional accountability. Public funding for education in the United States indicates widespread agreement that education is a public good that, at its best, produces numerous positive benefits for society. By the same logic, teaching should be considered a public act that ought to involve consideration of the larger public benefit above self-interest.

In practical terms, however, explicit provisions for client protection of the sort employed in the legal profession through client protection funds seem problematic in the context of education, given the differences in financial stakes and incentives discussed above. Finding means by which to encourage teachers to take a broader perspective on their practice and to become interested in advancing teaching and the public interest is a laudable goal, but it is worth considering whether demanding financial contributions from teachers would be effective in encouraging attention to the public interest above their own limited financial self-interest. Similarly, requirements for *pro bono* work in a profession that may already demand large amounts of extra time for grading papers and preparing lessons may not be an effective way to ensure a stronger sense of professional responsibility among teachers.

Alternative means of promoting professional responsibility in education might be more promising. Accountability in education might focus on building a sense of collective responsibility for student outcomes among teachers in a school, district, or state by using positive incentives for group work rather than collective punishment for poor individual performance. For example, widening teachers' interests beyond their own classrooms by increasing teacher participation in schoolwide decisionmaking or by creating more opportunities for collective planning, team-teaching, and mentoring, and then linking performance incentives to schoolwide outcomes, might help to foster a wider sense of professional responsibility within schools. Similar programs could perhaps be scaled up to the district or state level, as well.

Educators Would Need Methods of Self-Policing and Self-Regulation

The idea of self-policing is not new to leaders in education. In writing about the inherent nature of professions, former American Federation of Teachers President Albert Shanker includes among his criteria that a true profession should "evaluate the performance of practitioners and remove from the profession those whose performance fall below standards" (AFT, 2000). In practice, however, teacher discipline involves little in the way of self-regulation. In a few states, professional standards boards do include certified teachers and have the power to investigate and prosecute disciplinary cases. In most cases, though, investigation is carried out by local school boards, staff from the state department of education, or state's attorneys (NASDTEC, 2002). Unlike the bar associations, which financially and logistically support the prosecution of accused attorneys, teachers' unions and professional organizations tend to support the accused defendant, often providing legal representation and support services throughout the disciplinary process. Despite rhetoric in support of self-policing, teachers' professional organizations have typically demonstrated little support for efforts to remove incompetent or unethical teachers from the profession.

The example of the legal profession suggests the possibility for a fairly radical restructuring of teacher disciplinary systems. Of course, educators could not institute such a model alone without considerable support from policymakers and the state. A model system might be administered by a panel of teachers and laypersons appointed by and responsible to the state department of education. Centralized complaint intake at the state level would simplify the system for parents. It could also reduce the burdens and pressures of serious disciplinary problems currently placed on school principals, allowing them to focus more on those complaints not warranting a full disciplinary hearing that could be referred back to the local level for mediation and nondisciplinary intervention. A prosecutorial branch would include certified teachers and staff attorneys working together to investigate complaints and prosecute cases of alleged misconduct before disciplinary panels made up of certified teachers and laypersons that would make recommendations for sanctions, although final decisions would remain in the hands of the state department of education.

Teachers' professional organizations would help to fund and administer the agency, recognizing that the removal of incompetent or unethical teachers serves the interest of the profession as a whole. This would be a significant departure from the status quo and might well prove to be the most difficult aspect of professional accountability to implement. On the one hand, union interests do not seem to require automatic protection of members against all accusations. Indeed, it is conceivable that a union's bargaining power might be strengthened if it could guarantee the competence of all of its members. On the other hand, if the promised provision of legal services as a membership benefit aids in union recruiting, it may prove difficult to transform teachers' organizations from self-protecting to self-policing entities. Professional organizations for teachers may well be performing a vital service in providing legal services in defense of teachers who could not otherwise navigate the often complex system of disciplinary hearings, in contrast to lawyers who, as discussed above, are well-prepared for the role of defendant.

Finally, given the credibility issues facing the disciplinary system for lawyers, educators must do more than simply imitate the legal profession. Rather, if professional accountability in education is to gain credibility, the disciplinary system for teachers must raise the bar and be a standard-bearer for effectiveness in dealing with public complaints in a satisfactory manner.

Professional Accountability Is Complemented by Market Accountability

It is important to recognize that lawyers face other types of accountability in addition to professional accountability. Although the legal profession relies on the system of professional accountability to distinguish between the competent and the incompetent and between the ethical and unethical, it also allows the forces of the market to hold lawyers to account and to make finer gradations among the competent and the good.

By contrast, many scholars and policymakers have noted that the teaching profession is generally quite insulated from market pressures. Creating more freedom for school and district administrators to hire and release staff as they see fit, and simultaneously increasing competition among schools and/or districts through choice reforms would help bring teaching more in line with the legal profession's dual system. Although some voices with very different views on accountability in education have suggested that market and professional accountability make poor partners (Finn, 2002; O'Day, 2002), the example of the legal profession suggests that in fact they may complement each other quite well.

CHAPTER SIX

Clinical Practice Guidelines in the Health Sector

Marjorie Pearson and Brian Stecher

In the health care industry, clinical practice guidelines serve as outlines of best practices for treating specific medical conditions. Independent organizations create these guidelines to support clinicians in their decisions on patient care. The guidelines are not mandatory, but clinicians who use them do so with the understanding that guideline practices are based on scientific evidence and expert judgment. The purpose of clinical practice guidelines is to improve the quality and efficiency of care. In this chapter, we explain how practice guidelines are developed and how they are used in the health care industry. We then explore how similar types of guidelines might be used in education.

Background

Health care guidelines come from many different organizations. In 1989, the U.S. federal government created the Agency for Healthcare Research and Quality (AHRQ)[1] to support the development of clinical practice guidelines and promote health outcomes research. The American Medical Association (AMA), other physician organizations, and medical specialty societies (e.g., the American Diabetes Association) also produce practice guidelines.

---

[1] Originally called the Agency for Health Care Policy and Research (AHCPR).

Medical practice guidelines vary in format and specificity, but they are usually specific statements that characterize the patients to whom the guidelines apply and a recommended course of action. The organization that developed the guideline often indicates the strength of their recommendation and/or the strength of the evidence supporting the recommendation. Two brief examples illustrating these features from the National Guideline Clearinghouse (http://www.guidelines.gov, accessed May 30, 2003) are as follows:

> **Guideline:** Post-mastectomy radiotherapy is recommended for patients with four or more positive axillary lymph nodes (II level of evidence, B grade of recommendation). Developed by the American Society of Clinical Oncology.

> **Guideline:** Asymptomatic women ages 40–49 should be offered screening with mammography every one to two years. These women should be: 1) informed of the benefits and harms of mammography; and 2) encouraged to make a personal decision, in collaboration with their physician, about whether to be screened and how frequently (evidence-based). Developed by Kaiser Permanente, Southern California.

Health Care Guideline Development

Developing clinical practice guidelines involves four basic steps: (1) selection of an appropriate topic; (2) selection of the panel or group of people who will make the guideline decisions; (3) collection and presentation of the information on which the guideline decisions will be made; and (4) the decisionmaking process itself. To be effective, the guidelines then must be implemented in ways that influence the practice of medicine.

Topic Selection

Topics are frequently selected on the basis of cost, numbers, and practice variation. The medical conditions that are most common, expensive to treat, and subject to treatment variation are typically targeted for guideline development. The guidelines most commonly address the technical aspects of care but may cover the psychosocial aspects as well. For example, guidelines may suggest that patient choice be an important part of the clinician-patient interaction.

Identification of Decisionmaking Group

Selecting those responsible for generating the guideline recommendations is an important step in the process. Relevant professional and lay organizations are often asked to nominate individuals for a guideline development panel, and nominees may be subject to further screening based on their credentials, open-mindedness, and teamwork effectiveness. Selection typically is designed to avoid domination by one group or interest to avoid territorial, intellectual, or financial biases. A balanced representation may be actively sought among professions (e.g., physicians, nurses, allied health professions, and healthcare consumers), generalists and specialists, academic and clinic-based practice, geography, gender, ethnicity, and practice styles (e.g., clinicians who do and do not perform invasive procedures). For example, the Depression Guideline Panel, convened by the Agency for Health Care Policy and Research (renamed AHRQ), was composed of seven physicians (four with specialties in psychiatry and three with specialties in general internal or family medicine), one psychologist, one psychiatric nurse, one social worker, and one consumer representative (Depression Guideline Panel, 1993). The committee that developed the American Academy of Orthopaedic Surgeons knee injury guideline, on the other hand, was composed of seven orthopaedists.

Gathering the Evidence

The heart of guideline development is deciding which practices to recommend for given situations. Guideline developers must first identify the practices that produce the best outcomes, which are usually defined in terms of the greatest benefit to patients. The two most important questions are (1) What are the best outcomes to strive toward? and (2) Which processes produce these outcomes?

Appropriate practices are identified using both scientific evidence and expert opinion, with increasing emphasis on scientific evidence. Assessment of the scientific evidence should involve extensive literature review, evaluation of the quality of the studies, and synthesis of the findings. Recommendations may be graded or ranked by the strength of the evidence.

Although scientific research on the relationship between the processes and outcomes of health care has progressed rapidly in the past two decades, it still does not address the majority of clinical circumstances. Thus, expert opinion is an important means for identifying the practices appropriate for guideline recommendations.

Decisionmaking Process

Since any group of individuals is likely to present a diversity of opinion on a given topic, a method is needed to synthesize the diverse judgments. In the health field, such a method is commonly referred to as a consensus development method. While an informal approach may be used (e.g., a committee meeting), a more formal approach may provide the advantage of overcoming biasing influences in relatively unstructured group interactions (such as domination by one or two individuals).

The most thoroughly scientifically validated consensus development method in health care (although not commonly used) is one called the modified Delphi method, pioneered by the RAND Corporation in the 1970s (Murphy, Black, et al., 1998; Brook, Chassin, et al., 1986). After agreeing on a set of scenarios defining the factors that need to be considered in treatment decisions, panelists are asked to rate different treatment options for each scenario, both before and after group discussions, utilizing literature reviews, instructions, and rating sheets provided. This method allows the researchers to calculate both the appropriateness of the treatment method and the level of agreement among panelists.

Dissemination of Guidelines

The organization that developed the guidelines usually disseminates them to the target audience. The AMA also monitors and disseminates guidelines from various organizations and publishes them annually in its *Clinical Practice Guidelines Directory*, which currently lists approximately 2000 guidelines (AMA, 2000). In 1997, the AHRQ, AMA, and the American Association of Health Plans joined forces to create an online database of existing guidelines. The National Guideline Clearinghouse (http://www.guidelines.gov) provides extensive information on clinical practice guidelines. The guidelines are classified by disease, treatment, and the organization responsible for development.

The Effect of Guidelines on Health Care Practices

Evaluations of the effect of consensus recommendations on practice behavior suggest that it is difficult to translate guideline recommendations into everyday practice. Guideline dissemination alone has little effect on provider behavior. However, greater change occurs when the recommendations are implemented using behavioral change interventions and systems supports. Guidelines must be translated into practice through consensus building, quality improvement initiatives, changes in institutional policies and structures, implementation tools and strategies, setting of standards, monitoring and evaluation, and updating. The health care industry is increasingly encouraging guideline compliance through such prompting mechanisms as flowcharts, guideline pocket cards, and electronic reminders. Researchers have found strong evidence that guidelines, when effectively implemented, can change clinical practices and improve patient outcomes (Grimshaw, Freemantle, et al., 1995).

Guidelines also help to inform patients of their options for treatment and the kinds of care to expect. A number of clinical practice guidelines, the AHCPR-sponsored guidelines for example, include versions for the consumer as well as for the practitioner.

Applying the Concept of Practice Guidelines to Education

Health care guidelines were developed to improve the quality of clinical decisions by providing a focused, expert synthesis of relevant scientific knowledge and practice in a highly usable format. Conceivably, educators could benefit from an analogous concept to guide instructional practice. Teachers could benefit from instructional guidelines that help them improve decisions about how to structure learning environments, develop lessons, prepare assignments, and interact with students in pursuit of specific learning objectives in specific contexts. For example, what should a teacher do to help a second grade student who continues to be confused about place value after a series of lessons presenting the concept using counters and base-10 blocks?

Ideally, expert teachers, utilizing empirical research evidence, could agree on important diagnostic questions that need to be asked and a set of instructional alternatives that would follow from each. Or, what might a middle school English teacher do when student essays are wildly off-topic? Again, expert guidance should be able to give suggestions for diagnosing potential problems and addressing them, e.g., providing models for essay prompts that communicate more clearly the desired results. Parents would benefit from a consumer-friendly version of these guidelines to help them evaluate the extent to which their children's educational experiences are consistent with recommended practices.

Although most health care guidelines relate to technical medical decisions, some focus on aspects of health education. This suggests that educators might be able to develop guidelines for a range of educational practices. Here is a brief summary of a guideline related to health counseling.

> **Guideline.** The U.S. Preventive Services Task Force (USPSTF) recommends intensive behavioral dietary counseling for adult patients with hyperlipidemia and other known risk factors for cardiovascular and diet-related diseases. Intensive counseling can be delivered by primary care clinicians or by referral to other specialists, such as nutritionists or dieticians (B recommendation). (http://www.guidelines.gov, accessed May 30, 2003)

This guideline is accompanied by brief descriptions of the evidence supporting the recommendation and clinical considerations regarding dietary assessments, effective interventions combining nutrition education with behaviorally oriented counseling, the intensity of dietary counseling, office-level systems supports, and the possible harms of dietary counseling.

Education guidelines might follow a format similar to medical guidelines. The guideline might recommend certain strategies for teaching place value to second graders who are confused about the topic. It also might provide a short description of the research on these strategies, as well as the research on effective implementation of these strategies, their necessary intensity, and school-system supports. Other details, such as the appropriate instructor or setting (e.g., the regular teacher in the second grade class and/or a referral to a specialist) would be included, if indicated in the research evidence.

Similar steps could also be used to develop educational guidelines. The scientific evidence base for effective education strategies would need to be extensively expanded. Systematic processes would need to be developed for (1) selecting the instructional topic to address; (2) selecting the people to review the evidence and make the guideline recommendations; (3) specifying the outcomes of greatest interests and then collecting, reviewing, and synthesizing the studies that examine the relationship between educational practices and these outcomes; and (4) making decisions on the content and wording of the recommendations. An independent research institution would be well suited to the tasks of facilitating the implementation of these processes and providing the extensive technical assistance needed (e.g., literature review and synthesis of findings). NCLB requires all states to adopt standards that delineate specific learning objectives by subject and grade level; these might serve as a starting point for developing best-practice instructional guidelines.

Implications for Education

Practice Guidelines Could Address Variations in Teaching Practices

Recent investments in the development of clinical guidelines in health care were justified by concerns about the cost of health care and evidence of widespread variations in care. The argument for developing guidelines in education can be made on the basis of similar claims about the cost of poor student achievement and widespread variation in the qualifications, experience, and practices of teachers. Educational policymakers are beginning to confront publicly the fact that not all teachers have the skills and knowledge necessary to address the instructional challenges they face. In fact, those students most in need of good teaching are most likely to have inexperienced, underqualified teachers who could benefit from a compendium of effective practices designed to address specific problems in teaching and learning.

Guideline Development Would Be Limited by the Lack of Scientific Evidence

The model followed in health care could serve as a basis for guideline development in education, although modifications would be necessary to reflect the differences between the state of knowledge and practice in the two fields. Costs, the numbers of people affected, and educational practice variations could reasonably be considered in deciding which topics to select for developing education guidelines. Decisionmaking panels in education would require explicit selection criteria and balanced representation just as they do in health. Formal consensus development approaches would work similarly in both fields.

A major difference is the limited range of scientific evidence about appropriate instructional strategies. For the most part, teaching and learning have not been subject to the same experimental testing that supports the treatment of disease and injury. Nevertheless, experimentation is quite common in some educational domains, such as the teaching of reading, and syntheses about effective practice are emerging (although hotly contested). Such domains could serve as a starting place for guideline development. As in health care, expert opinion could be used to identify practices appropriate for guideline recommendations in areas lacking scientific evidence. Focusing on educational guideline development also might generate increased funding and support for best-practices research in this field.

Educators Need a Common System of Classification to Develop Guidelines

Another key difference between health care and education is the lack of a system of classification for describing learning needs. Although educational activities may be categorized by grade level and subject, there is no descriptive system in education comparable to the classification of diseases and health problems that exists in medicine. However, educators have done much to develop a language for talking about their practice. For example, the job analyses that support teacher-licensing examinations, such as Praxis, are one step in this direction, and the work of the National Board for Professional Teaching Standards to describe exemplary teaching practices is another. With modifications, these might serve as a basis for developing a common language and classification system to discuss problems in educational practice.

Without a system of classification, it is more difficult to diagnose problems. Consequently, education has not developed a diagnostic system as thorough as the one in medicine. Much work has been done to improve the quality of classroom assessment, however, which could lead to better diagnoses, especially if standard assessment models are widely adopted.

CHAPTER SEVEN

Risk Adjustment Methods in Health Care Accountability

Marjorie Pearson and Brian Stecher

Risk adjustment is used to hold providers accountable only for their own care-giving actions and not for patient characteristics beyond their control. In health services, risk adjustment means taking account of factors patients bring with them—factors that are independent of the medical treatment—that affect their *risk* of experiencing a good or bad outcome following treatment. Risk-adjustment methods attempt to isolate the effect of the care provided from that of other factors, such as the patient's age, the diagnosis, the severity of the condition, or other conditions occurring along with the condition being treated. In this chapter, we describe the risk-adjustment process in health care, its limitations, and the possibilities for using risk-adjustment in education.

Making Fair Comparisons

A quality monitoring and reporting system that compares health providers' outcomes requires a risk-adjustment system. The goal of this system is to control for the effects of different initial patient characteristics when making provider-to-provider comparisons. The goal is also described as "leveling the playing field" among the providers whose outcomes are compared (Iezzoni, 1994). A well-designed risk-adjustment system can minimize the incentives for a provider to prefer one patient over another for purposes of demonstrating quality. Risk adjustment can make it just as easy to demonstrate quality care with a difficult-to-treat patient as with an easy-to-treat patient. Similarly, risk adjustment works to prevent outcome reporting from unfairly damaging the reputation of a provider who serves a disproportionate share of difficult-to-treat patients.

Without risk adjustment, performance information can be inaccurate and misleading. A provider who cares for large numbers of terminally ill patients, for example, may appear to provide poor-quality care when measured by patient mortality if the terminally ill patients' increased risk of death is not taken into account. Inaccurate performance assessment, in turn, could lead providers to shy away from providing services to the terminally ill in favor of persons with a very low risk of death. Health outcomes that may be risk-adjusted include mortality, health-related quality of life, functional status, disease incidence, patient satisfaction with the care received, and resource utilization or costs of care. Risk adjustment can also be used in reimbursing providers for care given.

How Risk Adjustment Is Done

The essential steps in developing a risk-adjustment model are the following: (1) agree on the outcome of interest; (2) identify what predicts this outcome; (3) select the risk factors to be adjusted for; (4) operationalize these risk factors; and (5) combine them into a statistical regression model or method of adjustment.

The design of a risk-adjustment procedure begins with the identification of outcomes, since the specifics of the risk-adjustment approach are likely to vary with the outcome under study. Different factors may be taken into account depending on whether the purpose is to predict resource consumption for reimbursement, or to monitor and compare clinical outcomes, or to analyze treatment effectiveness (Iezzoni, Shwartz, et al., 1996).

After identifying the outcome to be studied—which might be death, poor quality of life, consumer dissatisfaction, or high costs—the analyst identifies the factors or preexisting conditions that independently affect this outcome and are not affected by the providers whose performance is being assessed. For example, analyses of the quality of care frequently adjust for age because research findings show that, for certain outcomes, the probability of a poor outcome increases with age (and age itself is not modifiable by the physician or health system). The principal diagnosis, e.g., HIV-AIDS, pneumonia, diabetes; the severity of this diagnosis; and the number as well as the severity of coexisting illnesses are risk factors for many health outcomes and are frequently adjusted for in analyses. Some outcomes are differentially affected by the patient's gender, race, ethnicity, income, geographic area of residence, functional abilities, social support, and treatment preferences. Analysis of the provider's effect on those outcomes would benefit from adjusting for these variables.

Identification and selection of risk factors involve expert judgment and review of the scientific literature on predictors of particular outcomes. This process is often followed by consideration of existing risk-adjustment models previously developed for similar patients or statistical analysis of a selected data set. An existing model may be used directly or may be recalibrated to better fit the population represented by the data.

Selecting those risk factors to include in the risk adjustment (from all risk factors identified) involves both practical and strategic considerations. On the practical side, data accuracy, completeness, and availability are key. Many risk-adjustment systems rely solely on secondary administrative data, such as computerized hospital discharge data or Medicare billing data. Such data are readily available, broadly inclusive, and relatively inexpensive. Other systems include numerous primary clinical variables, which must be obtained from medical record abstraction. Such systems are more clinically valid and more expensive.

On the strategic side, the factors selected—the independent variables in the model—should make sense to the people involved in the processes under study. In health, this criterion is referred to as *medically meaningful* (Iezzoni, 1994), which means that the risk factors are in fact linked to the outcome of interest and that the clinicians involved recognize these links. Other issues involved in the selection of risk factors in health include the timing of risk adjustment;

for instance, whether to include any variables after the patient's initial contact with the health system.

Health researchers struggle with the question of how many risk factors to include in the model. Some research suggests that increasing the number of risk factors may bring only limited marginal improvement in the model's performance. A recommended approach is to focus on collecting accurate and complete data on a small number of the most important variables (Ivanov, Tu, et al., 1999; Tu, Sykora, et al., 1997).

Both the development of the model and the adjustment itself rely on statistical regression techniques. To develop the model, the variable for the outcome of interest is used as the dependent variable (y) and the potential risk factors constitute the independent variables (x). When the dependent variable is dichotomous, as is often the case (e.g., mortality), logistic regression techniques are utilized. The beta coefficients from the model are use as weights, which are applied to individual patient data to predict expected outcomes. These individual probabilities are then averaged at the provider level (e.g., hospital or physician) to give that provider's *expected* outcome rate. The provider's *actual* outcome rate (e.g., how many deaths actually occurred) is then compared to the *expected* rate, and the relationship (e.g., the difference) between these two rates forms the basis for assessing the quality of that provider's performance.

Limitations

Risk adjustment is a necessary but problematic element in measuring and comparing health care outcomes. Most risk-adjustment models still explain only a relatively small proportion of the variance in outcomes. Although the practice of risk adjustment offers a solution to one measurement problem, it raises other concerns. Some risk-adjustment models are hard to understand, and clinicians may find them difficult to accept, even when they are based on complete and accurate data (Iezzoni, 1991). Research also shows that different models applied to analysis of the same outcome on the same patients can lead to different judgments (Iezzoni, Shwartz, et al., 1995; Iezzoni, Shwartz, et al., 1996; Pine, Norusis, et al., 1997). For example, one study of stroke mortality rates applied 11 different risk-adjustment models to the same database of stroke patients from 94 hospitals. The authors found that the various models gave different results as to whether a hospital's death rate was higher or lower than expected when adjusted for patient risk (Iezzoni, Shwartz, et al., 1995). It also should be noted that risk adjustment does not address a fundamental limitation of using outcomes comparisons in quality improvement efforts. When differences are detected among providers, it unfortunately is not always clear what processes should be changed to improve the outcome. Since there are many, many steps in an area such as surgery, simply knowing that the mortality rate for a particular surgery is higher at one hospital than another does not always indicate to the hospital administrators and clinicians what steps should be taken to improve the situation.

In spite of its flaws, risk adjustment is considered necessary in the health care industry. It enables organizations to use data on health outcomes to motivate improvement and to protect providers from being penalized for treating high-risk patients. It is intended to remove one source of variation in patient outcomes in order to estimate the quality of care more closely. Recognition of its limitations points to the importance of focusing on processes as well as outcomes of care in quality analysis and improvement.

Applying Risk Adjustment to Education

Health care and education face a similar challenge: how to measure performance and hold practitioners and organizations accountable when those who receive their services arrive with such a wide range of preexisting characteristics. Evaluating the quality of educators' performance on the basis of student test outcomes is likely to be inaccurate and misleading if the performance information is not somehow adjusted for differences in the initial conditions of the students. Furthermore, using outcomes measures alone in an accountability system could encourage educators to shy away from teaching those students who are most in need of good teaching or are considered to be the most difficult to teach. Educators are aware of the problems associated with outcome measures, and they have been exploring a range of methods, including "value-added" models (described below), to solve it. Risk adjustment is another approach that may help them address the problem. However, the health care experience also shows that risk adjustment methods are complex, frequently costly, and imperfect. The disadvantages associated with risk adjustment may be even greater in the education context, where meaningful data on student risks may be less available (without considerable additional cost) and the selection and use of specific risk factors more controversial. For example, race, ethnicity, and family income are strong predictors of achievement and obvious choices as adjustment variables. Yet there is likely to be strong resistance to using those measures because of the implication that we might have lower expectations for certain groups. For all these reasons, educators face significant challenges in creating risk adjustment models for widespread use.

Current Uses of Risk Adjustment in Education

The test-based accountability system currently in use in California illustrates the full range of attitudes toward risk adjustment in the accountability context. Schools in California receive an Academic Performance Index (API) based on the unadjusted scores of students on the Stanford Achievement Test, Version 9 (SAT-9). Schools are grouped into deciles based on their API scores and assigned a rank from 1 to 10. In addition, schools are assigned a second decile rank based on their performance in comparison to "similar schools." These schools are determined by a regression-based formula that predicts SAT-9 scores from student demographic characteristics. In this way, the system acknowledges both absolute and relative standing.

California also incorporates both perspectives in its formula for awarding cash bonuses to high-performing schools. The formula has elements that could be called progressive in that they reward gains among low-achieving students more than gains among high-achieving students. It also has elements that are neutral with respect to initial achievement, and it has elements that are regressive. For the purpose of computing an annual school improvement index, student test scores are grouped into five levels, and schools receive points for each student based on his or her level. The distribution of points is not uniform across levels, however, and the difference between levels decreases as the levels increase. Thus, a school receives more points for moving a student up from the bottom level to the next level than it does for moving a student up one level at the top of the scale. This is the progressive component. All scores are combined to generate the school API, which is the neutral component. The regressive component is that the criterion for qualifying for an award is tougher for schools with low initial achievement than for school with high initial achievement. The state has set an interim performance target of 800. All schools are expected to increase their API score by 5 percent of the distance to 800. Thus, schools at 700 have to show a five-point increase while schools at 600 have to show a ten-point increase. The net effect of the progressive and regressive elements of this system is so far unclear.

Other state accountability systems are not as complex as the one in California, but many have risk-adjustment features. Some states implicitly factor initial achievement differences into their accountability system by basing rewards on similar improvement rates rather than a sliding scale or absolute attainment. This approach acknowledges that student achievement is not distributed uniformly across schools, and it does not hold schools accountable for the characteristics of students upon entry.

NCLB represents a dramatic departure from this trend because it requires that all states adopt accountability systems that eschew explicit risk-adjustment mechanisms. The federal law mandates that schools must hold all students to the same standard regardless of their starting point. States must report progress separately for each subgroup (defined in terms of ethnicity, poverty, language, and disability), but all students are expected to demonstrate proficiency within 12 years. This eliminates the need for regression-based adjustments, but—more important—it establishes a very different standard for judgment. It remains to be seen how states like California will adapt their systems to comply with the federal rules and how the model of common standards will affect the conduct of educational research.

Finally, educators are beginning to use more-complex statistical techniques known as "value-added" models to estimate the average effect of teachers and schools on student achievement. These techniques use multiyear longitudinal achievement data linking teachers and students to estimate specific teacher and school effects. In essence, prior achievement serves as the basis for estimating the achievement increase associated with individual teachers and schools. This approach is being used in Tennessee to estimate the impact of individual schools. Tennessee uses results for individual teachers to plan professional development, but they are not used in performance reviews and are not made public. The models themselves are very complex and difficult to understand, and some of the statistical adjustments may even be counterintuitive. For example, in the Tennessee model the estimate for a teacher with a smaller class gets shrunk toward the mean more than the estimate for a teacher with a larger class. Although this is logical from a statistical point of view, it is difficult to explain, and teachers find it hard to accept that two classroom teachers who achieved the same average growth in student achievement would not have the same estimated effect. Nevertheless, many other states have expressed interest in adopting similar techniques.

These examples suggest that policymakers are of two minds when it comes to expectations for student outcomes. On the one hand, the recognition of individual differences is central to the educational enterprise. This leads to some acknowledgment that students pose different challenges, and judgments about success should recognize these differences. On the other hand, the rhetoric of standards captures an American ideal that all students should have equal opportunity. It would be unthinkable to set lower standards for groups of students based on their background or even on their initial level of attainment. The health care experience with risk adjustment offers little guidance as far as this dilemma is concerned. However, the health care analysis is relevant for the potential use of value-added estimates to judge individual teacher performance. When accountability begins to fall on individual teachers, there is likely to be far more sensitivity to arcane statistical issues, and educators would be wise to attend to the concerns raised by health care personnel described above.

Implications for Education

Risk Adjustment in Education May Be Controversial

In the area of educational accountability, attitudes about risk adjustment are complex. Education policymakers hold the somewhat contradictory beliefs that all students can learn to high levels and that some students have more difficulty learning and therefore present greater challenges to schools. The first belief leads to the establishment of high standards for all students and higher targets for schools whose average student performance is low. The second leads to systems that reward gains in achievement differently at different points in the distribution. Similarly, the first belief leads to policies that eschew risk adjustment, whereas the second leads to policies that incorporate some compensation for student differences. Applying risk adjustment in a broad context in education will require addressing the difference between these two approaches. Furthermore, race and ethnicity have traditionally been strong predictors of achievement (independent of family income), and therefore would be a logical choice as adjustment factors. However, this choice is likely to lead to controversy and intense political wrangling. Educators may be presently unwilling to engage in this debate.

Risk Adjustment Requires Agreement About Outcomes and Measures

In creating a risk-adjustment model, the first step is to specify the outcome of interest and how it will be measured. The outcome of interest in an educational context might be student attainment of academic standards adopted by the state, and mastery of the standards might be measured by standardized test scores. The purpose of risk adjustment would be to level the playing field so that teachers are held accountable only for those teaching processes under their control and not the factors outside of their control, such as student learning problems, or the initial achievement level of students when school starts. The process of setting standards and adopting tests is complex and involves a number of compromises, both political and technical. In most states, those judgments have already been made as part of the implementation of NCLB. Although they are not without controversy, all states now have adopted outcomes and measures as part of their NCLB accountability system. They have also established increasing annual performance targets for students, which, if met, will lead to universal proficiency by 2014.

Identifying Risk Factors Accurately Requires Extensive Data

The second step in creating a risk-adjustment model is identifying causal relationships; i.e., which factors best predict which outcomes. The selection of risk-adjustment factors will be a complicated issue for education, and data availability will be a prime consideration in education, as in health. An important difference between health and education is that large bodies of data on health risks have been collected through screening tests, physical exams, histories, diagnostic tests, etc. and documented in inpatient and outpatient medical records. Educators, however, do not have a similar body of risk data, and they face complicated access issues if they try to collect it. Among those issues are privacy protection and the costs of accessing, abstracting, and verifying accuracy. The risk data currently available in education may be inadequate to support a proposed accountability system. Policymakers should understand that such a system may demand substantial resources to gather the data needed to make it work.

Educators Should Understand and Accept the Risk-Adjustment Model

In health research, analysts understand that the risk factors selected should make sense to the stakeholders, and the same principle applies in education. The teachers and administrators whose performance is being evaluated should have a reasonable understanding of the risk-adjustment factors and their relationship to the test scores for the accountability and improvement system to be considered credible and accepted. This may require considerable training for teachers and administrators on the evidence underlying risk adjustment and the accountability system itself.

CHAPTER EIGHT

Health Care Report Cards and the Public Release of Data

Marc Chow and Brian Stecher

While there is no formal, industry-wide accountability system for health care, there are many mechanisms that promote accountability and process improvement. Health care report cards and the public release of data serve to inform consumers about the relative performance of the clinicians and hospitals from whom they may receive services. The public availability of performance data and the existence of market forces work together as informal improvement and accountability mechanisms in the health care industry. In this chapter, we discuss the history of health care report cards, how they have affected the industry, and how a similar mechanism might work in education.

Facilitating Improvement by Means of Information

Although there are many methods of measuring performance in health care, the industry has no formal accountability mechanism. State governments license physicians and accredit health care providers to protect public safety, but they neither measure performance systematically nor impose consequences as a result. There are no direct, causal links between performance data, health care providers, and consumers, and there is no regulation or official mechanism that translates these data into actions.

However, many organizations actively collect and disseminate information about the performance of selected components of the health care system. This information takes various forms, including "report cards," "consumer reports," "public performance reports," and "provider practice profiles." These reports summarize the performance of health providers with varying levels of specificity and detail. In most cases, performance is compared on a common set of indicators selected by the group or organization providing the report.

The organizations release performance data on the premise that the information will lead to improvements in the quality of health care. They believe that the more information that is available, the better prepared consumers will be to choose their health care providers and the more inclined health care providers will be to improve care. Research suggests that the availability of performance data may already have caused changes in provider behavior and improvements in both the process and outcomes of care (Marshall, Shekelle, Leatherman, et al., 2000).

History of Health Care Report Cards and Public Release of Data

Report cards and public access to performance data are relatively new to the health care industry. One of the first public releases of data occurred in the mid-1980s when the Health Care Financing Administration (HCFA) publicly released hospital-specific mortality rates for Medicare patients. In subsequent years until 1992, HCFA released reports identifying all community hospitals' actual and expected mortality rates.

Following the HCFA release, a number of states began to release information on the performance of hospitals and health care providers. New York and Pennsylvania were among the first states to systematically report data on health outcomes by institution or by physician. Both states focused their reports on a specific type of high-risk procedure, coronary surgery. The New York State Department of Health created the Cardiac Surgery Reporting System, which included severity-adjusted mortality rates by hospital, highlighting the difference between the institution and the state average and identifying those hospitals and surgeons with rates higher or lower than the statewide rates. New York also published a booklet on coronary surgery outcomes that provided the actual number of in-hospital deaths, observed mortality rates, expected mortality rates, and risk-adjusted mortality rates, by hospital and surgeon. In 1994, Pennsylvania released a report that included the total number of coronary bypass surgery patients and mortality data by individual physician, physician group, and hospital. Today, both New York and Pennsylvania have Web sites that contain information the public can access on a variety of health care issues.

More recently, the two main accrediting organizations in the health care market, the National Committee for Quality Assurance (NCQA) and the Joint Commission on Accreditation of Healthcare Organizations (JCAHO), have taken the lead in collecting and disseminating data on health providers. These reports contain data derived from the accreditation process, which reviews health plans against more than 60 different standards. Although this accreditation process is voluntary, some employers and group purchasers only offer NCQA-accredited health plans to their employees. This fact has pushed many large plans to become accredited by NCQA, making the data widely available. The standards focus on the structural aspects of the providers and fall into five major categories: access and service, qualified providers, staying healthy, getting better, and living with illness. The data are summarized in a common format and made available publicly.

NCQA also manages a separate performance measurement tool for the managed care industry known as the Health Plan Employer Data and Information Set (HEDIS). HEDIS started in the early 1980s as a joint effort by private purchasers and the managed care industry to develop a standardized set of performance measures that would provide comparative information for purchasers and consumers trying to choose among competing managed care plans. As the system has evolved, the collaboration has expanded to include public purchasers, including Medicare, Medicaid, and the state Child Health Insurance Program. HEDIS data are collected, analyzed, and reported at the health plan level. The 2000 version of HEDIS contains a set of more than 50 performance measures used to evaluate and compare health plans. At present, HEDIS is the most commonly used database for comparing health plans at the performance level.

NCQA also participates in a number of state and local report card projects. These projects have allowed it to create Quality Compass, a national database of HEDIS performance information and NCQA accreditation information drawn from hundreds of health plans. Quality Compass acts as a central repository for data and attempts to address the growing needs of employer purchasers, consumers, health plans, and others for access to reliable, standardized performance data. Health plans that do not go through the formal NCQA accreditation process are also allowed to submit data to Quality Compass. However, since submitting data remains voluntary, it is difficult to truly compare all health plans nationwide. Yet, employers and purchasers are able to use Quality Compass information to make decisions about which health plans they feel would best serve their employees' needs and interests. The Quality Compass reports also give consumers more information about their health plan choices. NCQA claims that nearly 100,000 people per month visit its Web site to search for information or use their "Health Plan Report Card" to research health plans in their area.

The Joint Commission on Accreditation of Health Care Organizations also has an accreditation process similar to the NCQA process. JCAHO has developed professionally-based standards and evaluates the compliance of health care organizations against these benchmarks. Recently, it has begun to broaden the range of indicators included in its accreditation process to include processes and outcomes as well as structural measures.

JCAHO believes that the use of outcomes-related data in accreditation activities will serve as a greater stimulus than the previous non-outcome measures for health care organizations to examine their processes of care and take action to improve the results of care. It is also developing formats for reporting on provider performance in standardized ways. On its Web site, JCAHO offers *Quality Check,* a comprehensive guide to all JCAHO-accredited health care organizations. *Quality Check* also provides performance reports that include information on the organization's overall performance level and how it compares to other organizations nationally in specific performance areas. Many private groups are also producing health care quality reports for business groups, purchasing coalitions, employers, and consumers in specific locations. One example of a business group that uses NCQA and JCAHO data to produce its own customized report is the Pacific Business Group on Health, a nonprofit coalition of employers dedicated to improving the quality of health care while moderating costs.

Finally, the media also have become more involved in reporting on health care. *Newsweek* annually publishes data ranking health plans in terms of satisfaction and accreditation, as well as "staying healthy," "getting well," and "living with illness." *U.S. News and World Report* also publishes regular performance reports on health care organizations. Ratings compiled by newspapers and newsmagazines may not be as rigorous or as detailed as those produced by the health care organizations mentioned above, but the media's role in the dissemination of reports is very important.

How Report Cards Have Affected the Health Care Industry

Health Care Organizations

Health care organizations seem to respond to health care report cards more than consumers and individual physicians do (Marshall, Shekelle, Leatherman, et al., 2000). Hospitals may use the information to change their practices or to market their organizations. For example, in one study, a hospital that received poor ratings stated that they "led administrators to examine and then change the medical staff members assigned to treating [certain] patients in the ER" (Rainwater et al., 1998). However, two-thirds of the hospital leaders in the study stated that they made no changes in patient care in response to the health care report card. Hospitals with better-than-expected outcomes may use reports as a marketing tool and distribute the information through brochures or newspaper advertisement.

Competition is an important factor in the use of report card results. Hospitals in competitive markets were twice as likely to implement changes in response to health care data as were hospitals in less-competitive markets (Longo and Daugird, 1994). Hospitals with higher mortality rates are more likely to receive negative publicity and fewer patients (Topol and Califf, 1994), and those with better outcomes are more likely to have increased market share and higher fees (Mukamel and Mushlin, 1998).

Physicians and Clinicians

Many physicians are interested but skeptical about the value of report card data. For example, physicians initially reacted defensively to plans to make medical information available to peer review organizations, insurers, patients, and the public (Topol and Califf, 1994). Physicians are concerned that the public release of data may threaten their autonomy, which some believe is a defining characteristic of the medical profession. They are also concerned that negative data could ruin a physician's reputation or career.

There is some evidence that physicians do change their behavior in response to the release of negative data (Topol and Califf, 1994). Overall, they seem to think that performance measures can provide a formal and objective approach to improving individual decision-making, which is a good thing. However, although physicians appear to accept reports for their own purposes, they do not necessarily favor *public* reporting.

Consumers

One justification for the public reporting of data is that consumers will make more-informed decisions on health care if they have more information about quality. Ironically, recent surveys have shown that most consumers do not use health care report cards (National Survey on Americans as Health Care Consumers, 2000; Epstein, 1998). Many reasons have been identified to explain the lack of use by consumers, including difficulty in understanding the data, lack of trust in the information, and problems obtaining timely access to desired information (Marshall, Shekelle, Davies, and Smith, 2003).

Yet consumers care about the quality of health care. Consumers appear to react to negative outcome data, choosing physicians with lower reported mortality rates over those with higher rates (Topol and Califf, 1994). Three-quarters of the people surveyed for the National Survey on Americans as Health Care Consumers (2000) believe that the government should require health care providers to report all serious medical errors and make the information publicly available. A similar percentage rejected concerns about protecting the privacy of patients and medical staff as reasons to withhold those data. Patients also seemed to be interested in information on the cost, benefits covered, quality of care, overall satisfaction, technical competence, the evaluation provided by physicians, and information on coordination and access to care.

Mixed Reactions to Health Care Data Reporting

The release of health care information has not been without criticism and concern. Some organizations worry that the public release of data will stifle reporting and thus impede corrective actions. Others criticize the release of data because most reports are not timely in relation to the collection of data (Rainwater et al., 1998). Critics also point to the fact that measures are incomplete, there is a lack of standardization, and many reports have inadequate risk-adjustment methods (Epstein, 1995). Clinician professional organizations are concerned about confidentiality and the release of data that might hurt the reputation of individual clinicians. Finally, some researchers worry that report cards have the potential to lessen the quality of care in areas that happen to be difficult to measure (Smith, 1995). This decline in quality could occur if the reporting of selected outcomes (those that can be measured with ease, accuracy, etc.) causes providers to shift resources from other areas to improve their status on the reported measures.

In addition, there are criticisms of specific reporting systems. For example, HEDIS imposes considerable cost and administrative burdens. Moreover, HEDIS was designed for making comparison among the features of health care systems, not for making improvements in quality, and its reports are not geared toward driving improvement. Similarly, there are concerns about Quality Compass. Because participation is optional, it is possible that only those health plans with outstanding performance will publicly release their data. Despite these concerns, the amount of data on the performance of the health care system that is released to the public continues to grow.

Public Release of Data in Education

In both health care and education, specially trained practitioners provide services to individuals to improve their quality of life. In this way, physicians working in hospitals are analogous to teachers working in schools, and health providers' experience with report cards can provide useful insights for educational policymakers. Of course, the two sectors differ in important ways. There is little choice in education. In health care, patients can often choose doctors or health plans; in education, students rarely choose teachers or schools. Consumer choice is the mechanism through which accountability works in health care, and the lack of choice in education may limit the appropriateness of comparisons between the sectors.

Performance data are publicly available in both sectors. Until recently, the public reporting of educational performance data, particularly test scores, was quite common, but the nature of the information differed from jurisdiction to jurisdiction. Many states make the reporting of test results as highly visible as possible. Newspapers regularly report the results of state testing programs at the school and district levels. The No Child Left Behind Act of 2001 requires that report cards be issued annually for every school, district and state. The report cards must describe how well students are performing in mathematics and reading, and they must summarize the qualifications of teachers. Thus, the law creates a common metric for judging the quality of schools. In most states, the public is already used to seeing test results reported in the newspapers, so there is a ready audience for the new report cards.

Implications for Education

Performance Report Cards Work Best with Competition

In health care, report cards have their greatest effect on producer organizations and individual professionals who are trying to maintain a competitive advantage. When low ratings are made public, organizations and professionals tend to improve their practices to improve their public image and remain competitive in their industry. However, there is less market competition in education, and so it is difficult to predict how widespread release of performance data might change behavior in schools. Because NCLB introduces more choice for consumers, it could encourage more schools and teachers to react directly to report cards on their schools.

Publicizing Performance Data May Have Undesired Consequences

There has been considerable research about the effects of the release of high-stakes test scores on school practices in a subset of states. In general, this research shows that schools refocus time and instruction on the aspects of curriculum that are measured and de-emphasize those subjects and those methods of presentation that are not measured. This may account, at least in part, for the increases in test scores that have accompanied most high-stakes testing programs. It is impossible to tell the extent to which the scores are inflated by these practices or the extent to which they reflect an actual improvement in achievement.

The main rationale for the public reporting of educational data has been to influence schools and teachers rather than to inform parental choice because school choice is more limited than health care choice. Under the 2001 amendments to the Elementary and Secondary Education Act, the penalty for consistently failing schools is to provide parents with the option of transferring their children to another school. This puts new power in the hands of consumers, and it may increase the leverage that public reporting has over educational providers.

There is little research on the effects of organizational report cards in education, and widespread access to data on educational quality is a relatively new phenomenon. One of the consequences of NCLB is likely to be a better understanding of the effects of school data on producers and consumers.

CHAPTER NINE

Conclusions

Brian Stecher and Sheila Nataraj Kirby

We undertook this exploration in the hope that we would gain useful insights into educational accountability by looking at accountability in other sectors. Many of the advocates on the national scene calling for greater accountability in education base their arguments on practices observed in the business sector. Our own knowledge of health care led us to believe that useful comparisons might also be found in this area. Conversations with colleagues suggested that educators could learn from accountability in the legal profession, in job training, and in other settings. Even so, we were surprised at the wealth and relevance of information contained in the models of accountability we chose to examine. We do not mean to imply that these models have worked perfectly in practice; indeed, as we have seen, each has its own limitations and drawbacks. Nonetheless, if the lessons learned from this investigation are applied cautiously and with due regard to limitations and contextual differences, we believe they offer useful direction for improving educational accountability.

The models presented in this monograph may help educators think about a number of specific issues, including how to make their goals and expectations clearer, how to use data as a basis for improvement, the utility of multiple measures that capture both process and performance (and the problems associated with narrowly defined measures of performance), the need to adjust output measures for the heterogeneity of inputs, how to establish standards for practice, and the elements of professionalization that may help teachers improve practice and reinforce personal accountability. Table 9.1 presents a

Table 9.1
Areas of Educational Accountability Where Non–Education Sector Models Offer Guidance

Areas	Malcolm Baldrige National Quality Award Program	Toyota Production System/ Lean Manufacturing	Job Training Partnership Act/ Workforce Investment Act	Legal Profession	Health Care Sector		
					Clinical Practice Guidelines	Risk-Adjustment Methods	Health Care Report Cards
Making expectations and goals clear	✓	✓	✓				✓
Using data for program improvement	✓	✓	✓				✓
Collecting multiple measures of performance and process	✓	✓	✓				✓
Adjusting performance measures for heterogeneity of inputs			✓			✓	
Improving instruction through standards of practice		✓		✓	✓		
Professionalizing teaching		✓		✓	✓		

cross-walk between the models discussed in the preceding seven chapters and the specific issues of educational accountability on which they offer guidance. Given the diversity of the models, the degree of concordance in the lessons learned for educators seems quite remarkable. For example, the Baldrige awards, TPS/Lean Manufacturing, and the JTPA/WIA cases all highlight the importance of clear expectations, using data for improvement, and collecting multiple measures of performance; both JTPA/WIA and the risk-adjustment methods used by the health care sector emphasize adjusting performance measures for the heterogeneity of inputs.

We encourage educators interested in these particular issues to review the information in the corresponding chapters.

Enhancing Effective Accountability in Education

The NCLB accountability system reflects a compromise among policymakers seeking to bring more-stringent controls to education. Some wanted greater parental choice; other wanted to place greater emphasis on the teacher's role. Some wanted to link performance on standardized tests to grade-level promotion; others wanted to broaden the assessment scheme to include open-ended and constructed-response questions. Negotiations over these and other issues led to the current system.

The accountability cases we studied offer insights into improvements that might enhance the current system. Some of the lessons point to specific details; others are broader in scope. For example:

- The JTPA/WIA example illustrates the potential benefits as well as the drawbacks of setting performance targets in terms of specific quantitative indicators. It demonstrates that, although quantitative targets influence the behavior of participants, their actions may well focus narrowly on the indicator rather than the broader outcome the indicator is designed to reflect. "Teaching to the test" is an example of this phenomenon. The JTPA/WIA example shows that using multiple indicators can reduce this tendency. The Baldrige model and the TPA/Lean Manufacturing model also emphasize the importance of collecting information about both process and performance.

- The JTPA/WIA example also suggests that performance targets should be sensitive to differences in client abilities upon entry, lest they distort the provisions of services. In response to a similar problem, the health care system uses risk-adjustment models to correct results for factors outside the control of physicians that influence patient outcomes. The risk-adjustment example illustrates how statistical techniques can be used to improve the fairness of comparisons when institutions serve different mixes of clients, but it also illustrates some of the limitations of these techniques. Some effort to condition educational performance targets based on initial differences in student performance would be consistent with experience in these sectors.

- The example of health care report cards shows that the public release of performance data can help drive improvements, through both internal and external pressures. Whether consumers exercise choice or not, the report card process creates pressures among providers that can be channeled into self-improvement efforts.

- The legal example extends our thinking about the basis for the accountability system. Professional standards can serve as a basis for accountability if there is a well-established knowledge base, if members of the profession can develop clear regulatory procedures, and if clients can exercise some choice. Professional accountability works in the legal profession because it is accompanied by market accountability.

These examples suggest a number of ways to think about improving educational accountability.

Broaden Performance Measures

Educators should be careful in setting performance objectives, understanding that they will drive behavior for better or worse. The current system measures performance almost exclusively in terms of reading and mathematics test scores. Educators need to be alert to the possibility that those scores are susceptible to manipulation through coaching, reallocation of instruction, test preparation, and other methods. Broadening "what counts" in the system is one way to diffuse the pressure to focus too narrowly and to deemphasize other important priorities.

Make Sure Performance Goals Are Fair to All Students and Schools

The accountability system should also make sure that the demands it places on schools and districts are fair, i.e., that they do not reward or penalize schools or districts for factors beyond their control. Given the wide variation in student characteristics and the limitations of risk-adjustment methods to statistically control for these differences when comparing outcomes, educators will continue to struggle with how to establish fair measures of performance. Moreover, the goal of fair comparisons must be balanced against the goal of closing the gap between successful and unsuccessful students. The latter concern may require placing unequal demands on schools to some degree. Negotiating between these opposing goals is an issue that the other sectors we studied have not confronted. Nevertheless, the experiences in JTPA/WIA and health point out the advantages of performance targets that are sensitive to initial inputs.

Develop Standards of Practice in Promising Areas and Encourage Professional Accountability

Although teachers often call for greater professional accountability, the conditions do not yet exist in education to replicate the legal or health care models. In particular, educators lack a codified knowledge base against which to judge their skills and performance, and educational consumers (students and parents) do not have the choices they have in the legal and health care arena. Movements to create more-explicit standards of practice would foster professional accountability and provide guidance to help schools and districts improve their performance. We encourage educators to select promising areas in which more-detailed practice guidelines might be developed. Such guidelines can form the basis for more-detailed standards for the teaching profession so that teachers can be more aggressive about monitoring their own professional competence. These steps would help broaden and deepen accountability in education. NCLB provides for limited parental choice, and this small step changes the conditions in education in a significant way. It is unclear, however, whether parental choice will ever operate in the same way as markets do in the professions.

Develop an Integrated, Comprehensive Strategy to Help Schools and Districts Improve Their Performance

Although NCLB formalizes on a national scale the identification of schools in need of improvement, the problem of underperforming schools is by no means a new one. The original Elementary and Secondary Education Act of 1965 was an attempt by the U.S. Congress to provide supplemental resources to enable schools serving large numbers of poor students to improve their educational offerings. States have also taken steps to identify poor schools and improve their operation. Unfortunately, most of the previous efforts to improve underperforming schools have not been successful. In general, the problems have proven to be beyond educators' capacity to solve. Furthermore, it is likely that, under the more stringent requirements of NCLB, even larger numbers of schools and school districts will be identified as in need of improvement. States and districts will need guidance on how best to provide such schools and school districts with assistance and resources to help them improve. The cases we studied provide examples of organizational self-improvement methods that could be applied to schools and districts. For example:

- The Baldrige example highlights the importance of self-assessment as a first step in organizational improvement and offers a systematic and strategic approach for bringing together processes, resources, and data to serve strategic goals. The Baldrige criteria have already been adapted for education, and some districts have begun to use them with success.

- The TPS example offers an alternative model in which improvement can arise from within, and it highlights the benefits of a system that empowers workers (in this case teachers) to study and continuously improve their practice, which could well lead to the development of a richer knowledge base about practice.

- The example of clinical practice guidelines highlights a potentially crucial missing piece in the educational improvement puzzle—guidance regarding effective teaching. It has taken the medical profession many years to synthesize experimental knowledge and produce recommendations regarding practices in specific situations. This is a potentially powerful example for educators to follow in systematizing their pedagogical knowledge base, which would contribute directly to improving school effectiveness. In addition, developing such standards of practice would promote the professionalization of teaching and foster the utility of professional accountability, as they have in the legal profession.

Taken together, these examples suggest that the key elements in an improvement strategy might include

- undertaking a focused institutional self-assessment (including asking the right questions and assembling the right kinds of information)
- understanding the school system as a linked process,
- developing and applying an expanded knowledge base about effective practice in varying situations
- empowering participants in the process (notably teachers) to contribute to improvement efforts.

Developing and adopting such a strategy in education will require time, effort, and a willingness to adapt principles from outside the educational sector. However, we believe that the key components of such a strategy have the potential to improve the performance of schools and school districts. Pilot efforts to adapt and test these components in diverse schools settings and focused efforts to create educational applications would be a good starting place to try to take advantage of the successful experiences of other sectors.

Final Conclusions

Overall, this investigation of accountability in other sectors sharpens our thinking about accountability in education. It suggests ways that educators can develop better strategies for improving the performance of schools and districts and that policymakers can redefine educational accountability to make it more effective. Educational performance would be enhanced if schools and districts had a repertoire of thoughtful procedures for self-study and improvement. The Baldrige and TPS models provide a good starting place for developing such methods—and there may be other models, as well. The experience of the health sector in developing clinical practice guidelines can help educators solidify a knowledge base essential to inform their instructional decisions.

The overall accountability system could be improved by broadening its focus to include indicators reflecting more of the public's goals for education. The system must not unfairly label schools and districts based on the characteristics of the students it serves while still maintaining pressure to raise the performance of those students at the bottom. A system based on measures of growth rather than one based on measures of status would be a move in this direction.

Finally, although education has much in common with business, law, and health care, it faces unique challenges that other industries do not face. Although it can learn from studying these other fields, in the end it will have to develop an accountability model that responds to its specific conditions.

References

Abbott, A. *The System of Professions: An Essay on the Division of Expert Labor.* Chicago, IL: University of Chicago Press, 1988.

Adams, J. E., Jr., and M. W. Kirst. New Demands and Concepts for Educational Accountability: Striving for Results in an Era of Excellence. *Handbook of Research in Education Administration.* Washington, DC: American Association of Educational Researchers, 1998, 463–489.

Adler, Paul S. Time-and-Motion Regained. *Harvard Business Review* (January–February 1993): 97–108.

American Bar Association Center for Professional Responsibility. *Lawyer Regulation for a New Century: Report of the Commission on Evaluation of Disciplinary Enforcement.* Chicago, IL: American Bar Association, 1992.

American Bar Association Section of Legal Education and Admission to the Bar. *ABA Standards of Approval for Law Schools.* Chicago, IL: American Bar Association, 2002.

American Bar Association Standing Committee on Professional Discipline. *Model Rules for Lawyer Disciplinary Enforcement: 2001 Edition.* Chicago, IL: American Bar Association, 2002.

American Bar Association Web site: http://www.abanet.org, accessed February, 2003.

American Federation of Teachers K–16 Teacher Education Task Force. *Building a Profession: Strengthening Teacher Preparation and Induction.* Washington, DC: American Federation of Teachers (AFT), 2000.

American Medical Association (AMA). *Clinical Practice Guidelines Directory: 2000 Edition.* Chicago, IL: American Medical Association, 2000.

Anderson, K., R. Burkhauser, J. Raymond, and C. Russell. Mixed Signals in the Job Training Partnership Act. *Growth and Change* (1992) 22(3): 32–48.

Babson, S. Lean Production and Labor: Empowerment and Exploitation. In Steve Babson (ed.), *Lean Work: Empowerment and Exploitation in the Global Auto Industry.* Detroit, MI: Wayne State University Press, 1995, 1–37.

Barber, B. Some Problems in the Sociology of Professionals. *Daedalus,* (1963) 92(4): 669–688.

Becker, Howard S. The Nature of a Profession. In Nelson B. Henry (ed.), *Education for the Professions: The Sixty-First Yearbook of the National Society for the Study of Education.* Chicago, IL: National Society for the Study of Education, 1962, 26–46.

Brook, Robert H., Mark R. Chassin, Arlene Fink, David H. Solomon, Jacqueline Kosecoff, and R. E. Park. A Method for the Detailed Assessment of the Appropriateness of Medical Technologies. *International Journal of Technology Assessment in Health Care* (1986) 2: 53–63.

Burk, J. Expertise, Jurisdiction, and Legitimacy of the Military Profession. In D. M. Snider and G. L. Watkins (eds.), *The Future of the Army Profession.* Boston, MA: McGraw-Hill, 2002, 19–38.

Carr-Saunders, A. M., and P. A. Wilson. *The Professions.* Oxford, UK: Oxford University Press, 1933.

Choi, T. Y. The Successes and Failures of Implementing Continuous Improvement Programs: Cases of Seven Automotive Parts Suppliers, In Jeffrey K. Liker (ed.), *Becoming Lean: Inside Stories of U.S. Manufacturers.* Portland, OR: Productivity Press, 1998, 409–456.

Collins, J. J., and T. O. Jacobs. Trust in the Military Profession. In D. M. Snider and G. L. Watkins (eds.), *The Future of the Army Profession.* Boston, MA: McGraw-Hill, 2002, 39–58.

Conference of Chief Justices Working Group on Lawyer Conduct and Professionalism. *A National Action Plan on Lawyer Conduct and Professionalism.* Conference of Chief Justices, 1999.

Cook, C. Review of *Lean Work: Empowerment and Exploitation in the Global Auto Industry,* edited by Steve Babson. *Work and Occupations* (1996) 23(3): 334–336.

Cook, C. R., and J. C. Graser. *Military Airframe Acquisition Costs: The Effects of Lean Manufacturing.* Santa Monica, CA: RAND Corporation, MR-1325-AF, 2001.

Courty, P., and G. Marschke. Measuring Government Performance: Lessons from a Federal Job-training Program. *AEA Papers and Proceedings* (May 1997) 87(2): 383–388.

_____. The JTPA Incentive System. In James Heckman (ed.), *Performance Standards in a Government Bureaucracy: Analytic Essays on the JTPA Performance Standards System.* Kalamazoo, MI: W.E. Upjohn Institute for Employment Research, forthcoming.

Cragg, M. I. *Performance Incentives in Government Subcontracting: Evidence from the Job Training Partnership Act (JTPA).* New York: Columbia University Department of Economics, 1995.

Darling-Hammond, Linda, and C. Ascher. *Creating Accountability in Big City School Systems.* New York, NY: National Center for Restructuring Education, Schools, and Teaching. ERIC Document Reproduction Service No. ED 334-339, 1991.

Darling-Hammond, Linda, and Peter Youngs. Defining "Highly Qualified Teachers": What Does "Scientifically-Based Research" Actually Tell Us? *Educational Researcher* (December 2002) 31(9): 13–25.

Day, J. C. Learning About Lean Systems at Freudenberg-NOK: Where Continuous Improvement Is a Way of Life. In Jeffrey K. Liker (ed.), *Becoming Lean: Inside Stories of U.S. Manufacturers.* Portland, OR: Productivity Press, 1998, 179–200.

Depression Guideline Panel. Depression in Primary Care: Volume 2. *Treatment of Major Depression. Clinical Practice Guideline, Number 5.* Rockville, MD: U.S. Department of Health and Human Services, Public Health Service, Agency for Health Care Policy and Research, AHCPR Publication No. 93-0551, April 1993.

Dingwall, R. Accomplishing Profession. *The Sociological Review* (1976) 24(2): 331–349.

Easton, George S., and Sherry L. Jarrell. The Effects of Total Quality Management on Corporate Performance: An Empirical Investigation. *The Journal of Business* (April 1998) 71(2): 253–307.

Eaton, A. The Role of the Union and Employee Involvement in Lean Production. In Steve Babson (ed.), *Lean Work: Empowerment and Exploitation in the Global Auto Industry.* Detroit, MI: Wayne State University Press, 1995, 70–78.

Epstein, A. Performance Reports on Quality—Prototypes, Problems, and Prospects. *New England Journal of Medicine* (July 6, 1995) 333(1): 57–61.

Epstein A. Rolling Down the Runway: The Challenges Ahead for Quality Report Cards. *Journal of the American Medical Association* (1998) 279 (21): 1691–1696.

Ernst and Young and American Quality Foundation. *International Quality Study: The Definitive Study of the Best International Quality Management Practices; Top-Line Findings.* Cleveland, OH: Ernst and Young, 1992.

Finn, Chester E., Jr. Real Accountability in K–12 Education: The Marriage of Ted and Alice. In W. M. Evers and H. J. Walberg (eds.), *School Accountability: An Assessment by the Koret Task Force on K–12 Education.* Stanford, CA: The Hoover Institution, 2002, 23–46.

Flexner, A. Is Social Work a Profession? In *Proceedings of the National Conference of Charities and Correction.* Chicago, IL: Hildmann Printing Co., 1915, 576–590.

Ghobadian, Abby, and Hong Seng Woo. Characteristics, Benefits and Shortcomings of Four Major Quality Awards. *International Journal of Quality & Reliability Management* (1996) 13(2): 10.

Gill, Brian P., P. Michael Timpane, Karen E. Ross, and Dominic J. Brewer. *Rhetoric Versus Reality: What We Know and What We Need to Know About Vouchers and Charter Schools.* Santa Monica, CA: RAND Corporation, MR-1118-EDU, 2001.

Goode, W. Community Within a Community: The Professions. *American Sociological Review* (1957) 22: 194–200.

Greenwood, E. Attributes of a Profession. *Social Work* (July 1957) 2: 45–55.

Grimshaw, J., N. Freemantle, S. Wallace, I. Russell, B. Hurwitz, I. Watt, A. Long, and T. Sheldon. Developing and Implementing Clinical Practice Guidelines. *Quality Health Care* (1995) 4: 55–64.

HALT Web site: http://www.halt.org/.

Hamman, D., and E. A. Schenck. Corrective Action and School Choice in NYC: An Analysis of District Funding Application. *Education Policy Analysis Archives* (2002) 10(45). http://epaa.asu.edu/epaa/v10n45.html, retrieved 10/21/02.

Heckman, J., and J. Smith. The Determinants of Participation in a Social Program: Evidence from JTPA. University of Chicago: unpublished manuscript, 1995.

Heckman, J. J., C. Heinrich, and J. Smith. The Performance of Performance Standards. In James Heckman (ed.), *Performance Standards in a Government Bureaucracy: Analytic Essays on the JTPA Performance Standards System.* Kalamazoo, MI: W.E. Upjohn Institute for Employment Research, forthcoming.

Heckman, J. J., J. Smith, and C. Taber. What Do Bureaucrats Do? The Effects of Performance Standards and Bureaucratic Preferences on Acceptance into the JTPA Program. In Gary Libecap (ed.), *Advances in the Study of Entrepreneurship, Innovation, and Economic Growth,* Volume 7, *Reinventing Government and the Problem of Bureaucracy.* Greenwich, CT: JAI Press, 1996, 191–218.

Hendricks, Kevin B., and Vinod R. Singhal. Does Implementing an Effective TQM Program Actually Improve Operating Performance? Empirical Evidence from Firms That Have Won Quality Awards. *Management Science* (September 1997) 43(9): 1258–1274.

Holmstrom, B., and P. Milgrom. Multitask Principal Agent Analyses: Incentive Contracts, Asset Ownership and Job Design. *Journal of Law, Economics, and Organics,* special issue (1991) 7: 24–52.

Iezzoni, L. L. (ed). *Risk Adjustment for Measuring Health Care Outcomes.* Ann Arbor, MI: Health Administration Press, 1994.

Iezzoni, L. L. "Black Box" Medical Information Systems: A Technology Needing Assessment (editorial). *Journal of the American Medical Association* (1991) 265(22): 3006–3007.

Iezzoni, L. L., M. Shwartz, A. S. Ash, J. S. Hughes, J. Daley, and Y. D. Mackiernan. Using Severity-Adjusted Stroke Mortality Rates to Judge Hospitals. *International Journal for Quality in Health Care* (1995) 7(2): 81–94.

Iezzoni, L. L., M. Shwartz, A. S. Ash, and Y. D. Mackiernan. Predicting In-hospital Mortality for Stroke Patients: Results Differ Across Severity Measurement Methods. *Medical Decision Making* (1996) 16(4): 348–356.

Ivanov, J., J. V. Tu, and C. D. Naylor. Ready-Made, Recalibrated, or Remodeled? Issues in the Use of Risk Indexes for Assessing Mortality After Coronary Artery Bypass Graft Surgery. *Circulation* (1999) 99: 2098–2104.

Johnston, Sarah Jane. How Toyota Turns Workers Into Problem Solvers. *Harvard Business School Working Knowledge* (November 26, 2001). Available at: http://hbswk.hbs.edu.

Kirst, M. W. *Accountability: Implications for State and Local Policy Makers.* Washington, DC: U.S. Department of Education, Office of Educational Research and Improvement, 1990.

Kraus, Jennifer M. Attorney Discipline Systems: Improving Public Perception and Increasing Efficacy. *Marquette Law Review* (Fall 2000) 81 (4): 273–300.

Lieberman, M. *Education as a Profession.* Englewood Cliffs, NJ: Prentice-Hall, 1956.

Liker, J. K. Introduction: Bringing Lean Back to the U.S.A. In Jeffrey K. Liker (ed.), *Becoming Lean: Inside Stories of U.S. Manufacturers.* Portland, OR: Productivity Press, 1998, 3–40.

Longo D. R., and A. J. Daugird. Measuring Quality of Care: Reforming the Health Care System. *American Journal of Medical Quality,* 1994 9(3): 104–115.

Marshall, M. N., P. G. Shekelle, H.T.O. Davies, and P. C. Smith. Public Reporting on Quality in the United States and the United Kingdom. *Health Affairs* (2003) 22(3): 134–148.

Marshall M. N., P. G. Shekelle, S. Leatherman, and R. H. Brook. The Public Release of Performance Data: What Do We Expect to Gain? A Review of the Evidence. *Journal of the American Medical Association* (2000) 283(14): 1866–1874.

Martindale-Hubbell Web site: http://www.martindale.com.

Millerson, G. *The Qualifying Associations: A Study in Professionalism.* New York: Humanities Press, 1964.

Mitchell, Ruth, and Patte Barth. *How Teacher Licensing Tests Fall Short.* Washington, DC: The Education Trust, 1999. http://www.edtrust.org.

Mukamel D., and A. I. Mushlin. Quality of Care Information Makes a Difference: An Analysis of Market Share and Price Changes After Publication of the New York State Cardiac Surgery Mortality Reports. *Medical Care* (1998) 36(7): 945–954.

Murnane, R. J., John B. Willett, and F. Levy. The Growing Importance of Cognitive Skills in Wage Determination. *The Review of Economics and Statistics* (May 1995) 77(2): 251–266.

Murphy, M. K., N. A. Black, D. L. Lamping, C. M. McKee, C.F.B. Sanderson, J. Askham, and T. Marteau. Consensus Development Methods, and Their Use in Clinical Guideline Development. *Health Technology Assessment* (1998) 2(3): i–iv,1–88.

National Association of State Directors of Teacher Education and Certification (NASDTEC). *2002 Manual.* Sacramento, CA: 2002.

National Conference of Bar Examiners (NCBE) and ABA Section of Legal Education and Admission to the Bar. *Comprehensive Guide to Bar Admission Requirements 2002*. Madison, WI: National Conference of Bar Examiners and American Bar Association, 2002.

National Conference of Bar Examiners. 2001 Statistics. *The Bar Examiner* (May 2002): 1–19.

National Guideline Clearinghouse Web site: http://www.guidelines.gov.

National Institute of Standards and Technology Web site: http://www.nist.gov/.

National Survey on Americans as Health Care Consumers: An Update on The Role of Quality Information. Kaiser Family Foundation and Agency for Healthcare Research and Quality, 2000.

Newmann, F., J. B. King, and P. Youngs. Professional Development That Addresses School Capacity: Lessons from Urban Elementary Schools. *American Journal of Education* (2000) 108(4): 259–299.

Nolo Web site: http://www.nolo.com.

O'Day, Jennifer. Complexity, Accountability, and School Improvement. *Harvard Educational Review* (Fall 2002) 72(3): 293–329.

O'Reilly, F. E. *Educational Accountability. Current Practices and Theories in Use*. Cambridge, MA: Harvard University, Consortium for Policy Research in Education, 1996.

Pannirselvam, Gertrude P., and Lisa A. Ferguson. A Study of the Relationships Between the Baldrige Categories. *International Journal of Quality and Reliability Management* (2001)18(1): 14–37.

Parker, M., and J. Slaughter. Unions and Management by Stress. In Steve Babson (ed.), *Lean Work: Empowerment and Exploitation in the Global Auto Industry*. Detroit, MI: Wayne State University Press, 1995, 41–53.

Pine, M., M. Norusis, B. Jones, and G. E. Rosenthal. Predictions of Hospital Mortality Rates: A Comparison of Data Sources. *Annals of Internal Medicine* (1997) 126(5): 347–354.

Powell, Thomas C. Total Quality Management as Competitive Advantage: A Review and Empirical Study. *Strategic Management Journal* (January 1995) 16 (1): 15–37.

Przasnyski, Zbigniew H., and Lawrence S. Tai. Stock Performance of Malcolm Baldrige National Quality Award Winning Companies. *Total Quality Management* (2002) 13(4): 475–488.

Rainwater J. A., P. S. Romano, and D. M. Antonius. The California Hospital Outcomes Project: How Useful is California's Report Card for Quality Improvement? The California Hospital Outcomes Project. *The Joint Commission Journal on Quality Improvement* (1998) 24(1): 31–39.

Rinehart, J., C. Huxley, and D. Robertson. *Just Another Car Factory? Lean Production and Its Discontents.* Ithaca, NY: Cornell University Press, 1997.

Ross, J. *Total Quality Management: Text, Cases, and Readings.* Delray Beach, FL: St. Lucie Press, 1993.

Roth, J. A. Professionalism: The Sociologist's Decoy. *Sociology of Work and Occupations* (1974) 1(1): 6–23.

Runte, Robert. Is Teaching a Profession? In Gerald Taylor and Robert Runte, (eds.), *Thinking About Teaching: An Introduction.* Toronto: Harcourt Brace, 1995.

Sandburg, C. The Lawyers Know Too Much. In Carl Sandburg and George Hendrick and Willene Hendrick (eds.), Selected Poems. San Diego, CA: Harvest Originals, 1996, 190–191.

Schneider. E., and A. M. Epstein. Use of Public Performance Reports: A Survey of Patients Undergoing Cardiac Surgery. *Journal of the American Medical Association* (1998) 279(20): 1638–1642.

Smith, P. On the Unintended Consequences of Publishing Performance Data in the Public Sector. *International Journal of Public Administration* (1995) 18(2&3): 277–310.

Snider, D. M., and G. L. Watkins. Introduction. In D. M. Snider and G. L. Watkins (eds.), *The Future of the Army Profession.* Boston, MA: McGraw-Hill, 2002, 3–18.

Spear, Steven, and H. Kent Bowen. Decoding the DNA of the Toyota Production System. *Harvard Business Review* (September–October 1999): 97–106.

Stecher, B. Consequences of High-Stakes Large-scale Testing. In Laura Hamilton, Brian Stecher, and Stephen Klein (eds.), *Making Sense of Test-Based Accountability in Education.* Santa Monica, CA: RAND Corporation, MR-1554-EDU, 2001.

Stecher, B., L. Hamilton, and G. Gonzales. *Working Smarter to Leave No Child Behind: Practical Insights for School Leaders.* Santa Monica, CA: RAND Corporation, WP-138-EDU, 2003.

Sterman, John D., Nelson P. Repenning, and Fred Kofman. Unanticipated Side Effects of Successful Quality Programs: Exploring a Paradox of Organizational Improvement. *Management Science* (April 1997) 43(4): 503–521.

Topol E. J., and R. M. Califf. Scorecard Cardiovascular Medicine. Its Impact and Future Directions, *Annals of Internal Medicine* (1 January 1994) 120(1): 65–70.

Tu, J. V., K. Sykora, and C. D. Naylor. Assessing the Outcomes of Coronary Artery Bypass Graft Surgery: How Many Risk Factors are Enough? *Journal of the American College of Cardiology* (1997) 30(5): 1317–1323.

U.S. Department of Education, Office of Postsecondary Education. *Meeting the Highly Qualified Teachers Challenge: The Secretary's Annual Report on Teacher Quality.* Washington, DC: U.S. Department of Education, 2002.

U.S. Department of Education. *School Improvement Report: Executive Order on Actions for Turning Around Low-Performing Schools.* Washington, DC: 2001.

U.S. Department of Labor Web site: http://www.doleta.gov.

U.S. General Accounting Office. *Management Practices, U. S. Companies Improve Performance Through Quality Efforts.* GQO/NSAID-91-190. Washington DC: 1991.

U.S. General Accounting Office. *Workforce Investment Act: Improvements Needed In Performance Measures to Provide a More Accurate Picture of WIA's Effectiveness.* Washington, DC: 2002.

The White House Web site: http://www.whitehouse.gov.

Winn, Bradley A., and Kim S. Cameron. Organizational Quality: An Examination of the Malcolm Baldrige National Quality Framework. *Research in Higher Education* (1998) 29(5): 491-512.

Womack, J. P., and D. T. Jones. Beyond Toyota: How to Root Out Waste and Pursue Perfection. *Harvard Business Review* (September-October 1996): 140–158.

Womack, J. P., D. T. Jones, and D. Roos. *The Machine that Changed the World: The Story of Lean Production.* New York: Harper Perennial, 1990.

Woolf, S. H., R. Grol, A. Hutchinson, M. Eccles, and J. Grimshaw. Clinical Guidelines: Potential Benefits, Limitations and Harms of Clinical Guidelines. *British Medical Journal* (1999) 318(7182): 527–530.

Woolson, D., and M. A. Husar. Transforming a Plant to Lean in a Large, Traditional Company: Delphi Saginaw Steering Systems, GM. In Jeffrey K. Liker (ed.), *Becoming Lean: Inside Stories of U.S. Manufacturers,* Portland, OR: Productivity Press, 1998, 121–160.

Zayco, M. J., W. M. Hancock, and D. J. Broughman. Implementing Lean Manufacturing at Gellman Sciences, Inc. In Jeffrey K. Liker (ed.),

Becoming Lean: Inside Stories of U.S. Manufacturers, Portland, OR: Productivity Press, 1998, 247–302.

Zemans, Frances Kahn, and Victor G. Rosenblum. *The Making of a Public Profession.* Chicago: American Bar Foundation, 1981.